"You do this for long enough, and you begin to crave originality like a desert wanderer craves cool clear water. Andrew Forbes's essays are cool and clear and may well slake the thirst of any thinking baseball fan."

"*The Only Way Is the Steady Way* turns Andrew Forbes loose as a writer, and what emerges is a collage of emotion and clever observation of baseball's larger meaning. His writing is poetic, imbued with nostalgia, and another reminder that baseball is the most literary of sports."

"Andrew Forbes writes so well about everything, with such a keen eye for detail and the texture of life, that you can sometimes forget that the occasion for these essays is baseball. And yet, there he always is, like a nimble infielder, with a fresh insight or deft turn on the game. There is no other writer working now whose baseball writing I admire more. This companion to *The Utility of Boredom* is a true gift."

T0160506

"Andrew Forbes's love of baseball is the most honest and difficult kind: clear-eyed, thoughtful, willing to see the flaws along with the beauty. This book is a beauty. Through the lens of Ichiro Suzuki's magnificent career, Forbes examines our potential and our prejudices, helping us see the times that make the game and the game that makes the times."

"You don't have to love (or even like) baseball to love *The Only Way Is the Steady Way*. Forbes' writing about baseball, something he's loved his entire life, transcends statistics, standings, highlight reels, and hype, and captures soul—not the soul of the game, but the soul of fandom. If you do love baseball, or have had any fond feelings about the game at some point in your life, you will find your feelings put into writing in the pages of this book. Baseball may not save the world, but this book will remind you that it does indeed matter."

# THE ONLY WAY IS THE STEADY WAY

# THE ONLY WAY IS THE STEADY WAY

## ESSAYS ON BASEBALL, ICHIRO, AND HOW WE WATCH THE GAME

### ANDREW FORBES

Invisible Publishing
Halifax & Prince Edward County

Library and Archives Canada Cataloguing in Publication

Title: The only way is the steady way : essays on baseball, Ichiro, and how we watch the game / Andrew Forbes.

Names: Forbes, Andrew, 1976- author.

Identifiers: Canadiana (print) 20200395467
                  Canadiana (ebook) 20200395645
                  ISBN 9781988784663 (softcover)
                  ISBN 9781988784748 (HTML)

Subjects: LCSH: Suzuki, Ichirō, 1973- | LCSH: Baseball.

Classification: LCC GV867 .F66 2021 | DDC 796.357—dc233

Edited by Andrew Faulkner
Cover and interior design by Megan Fildes | Typeset in Laurentian
With thanks to type designer Rod McDonald

Printed and bound in Canada

Invisible Publishing | Halifax & Prince Edward County
www.invisiblepublishing.com

Published with the generous assistance of the Canada Council for the Arts, the Ontario Arts Council, and the Government of Canada.

Canada Council    Conseil des Arts
for the Arts      du Canada

ONTARIO ARTS COUNCIL
CONSEIL DES ARTS DE L'ONTARIO
an Ontario government agency
un organisme du gouvernement de l'Ontario

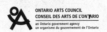
Canada

*For CC*

*Don't put him on a pedestal, just treat him with respect*
*He seeks but his own approval, and earns all that he gets.*

—"Ichiro Goes to the Moon," The Baseball Project

*Go, go, go, go, Ichiro*
*Rounding third and heading for home*
*Don't you know*
*Beats the throw*
*Dave says on the radio,*
*"Ichiro, you're unbelievable."*

—"Ichiro's Theme," Benjamin Gibbard

# AUTHOR'S NOTE

The majority of this book was written between early 2018 and late 2020. Given the requirements of the publication process the manuscript had to be fixed in place many months before its release date of April 2021. This is why you know things that I do not.

The book was perhaps three-quarters done when the novel coronavirus pandemic disrupted life on this planet, and so portions of the book were written when it was not clear whether or not there would be a baseball season in 2020. I recognize that a bat and ball game isn't of the highest importance in such times, but it certainly was of some concern as I tried to finish a baseball book. In the end baseball was played, albeit a shortened season with some strange rules (did they keep the strange rules?), with the stands full of cardboard cutouts. The playoffs were weird. The Dodgers won the World Series. I know that stuff, but as of this writing I still don't know what baseball might look like in 2021 and beyond.

The subjects of other references—such as who occupies the White House—are in flux this very minute. I know Joe Biden was fairly and resoundingly elected, for example, but I don't know how they finally got 45 out of the building. I know there is promising news about vaccines, but I don't know if and how they might allow us to get back to some semblance of a normal life.

Of perhaps greater significance to the content herein, the structure of Minor League Baseball is, as I type, undergoing a massive overhaul. Many teams have yet to finalize their affiliations, and other small-town teams are in danger of disappearing altogether. The majority of these essays were written under a now-obsolete system, and their content reflects that old way of doing things.

These will all be footnotes in future histories. Baseball—a game which daily reiterates its lessons of patience, persistence, and humility—will roll on, somehow. I'm certain of that. The game is something I have needed very much during the long months of lockdown and isolation. The strange mix of anxiety and boredom which has characterized the pandemic could, I found, be kept temporarily at bay by watching or listening to baseball, even when decades-old games were all that was available.

I can't say what kind of world will greet the release of this book. Happily, the larger subject of this volume is the purity of effort, and that's a subject without an expiration date, and impervious to the news cycle. I'm hopeful that there are sunny days ahead when we can gather in person and watch baseball, and share our love of it together.

—*AF, Peterborough, November 2020*

The last truck rolled out of Corktown bearing the remains of Tiger Stadium in September of 2009. Detroit's American League team had played at the corner of Michigan and Trumbull Avenues for better than a century, beginning in Bennett Park in 1896, and then in its replacement, Tiger Stadium, from 1912 until September 27, 1999. In that final game, the Tigers beat the Royals on a warm, cloudy afternoon, and then dug up home plate. It was transported a couple of miles east to their new downtown stadium, which bore the name of a financial services company, and featured a Ferris wheel and a carousel on its spacious concourse.

The ten years between that final game and the ballpark's demolition saw the city of Detroit sink deeper into the debt, corruption, and depopulation that had begun with the White Flight of the late 1960s, and were exacerbated by the oil crisis of the 1970s, and the exodus of auto industry jobs in the 1980s. The city bled jobs and revenue, discontinued services to whole neighbourhoods, and eventually became the largest American city to ever declare bankruptcy. In the midst of this state of crisis, the question of what to do with Tiger Stadium never figured prominently in the public discourse. There were those, including former Tigers broadcaster Ernie Harwell, who lobbied for preservation, but their pleas were met with a collective shrug, as though everyone thought it was someone else's issue to resolve. When the city finally awarded the demolition contract in early 2008, it looked like the fulfillment of an inevitability.

In 2003, Christie and I took a short trip around Lake Erie. We were not yet married and had no children. It was just us, a sedan, a couple backpacks, a tent, and sleeping bags. We ended up in Detroit and bought tickets to see the Tigers play Cleveland. Hours before game time we stood just north of the new stadium, overlooking the wide concrete trench of the Fisher Freeway, gazing out toward the Brush Park and Cass Corridor neighbourhoods on the far side. Christie, who is a biologist by training and temperament, is not a person given to overstatement. She grasped the chipped and corroded railing next to the sidewalk, high above the cars flying by on I-75, and surveyed the hollowed-out shells and boarded-up windows of dying city sectors.

"It looks like Sarajevo," she said.

→→→)《《←

When I was eight years old, I was convinced I would die in a nuclear holocaust.

My father, a naval officer who was frequently liaising in an official capacity with NATO and who was therefore in a position to know such things, listened patiently as I asked him if all the popular cultural attention paid to the nuclear threat—the songs and music videos and television shows and made-for-TV movies—was warranted.

He exhaled, weighing the potential impact of his words, performing the mental napkin math that all parents are called upon to calculate from time to time, to determine whether the value of truth is greater than the value of innocence.

"Yes," he finally said. "The threat is very, very real."

This was sometime in 1984. Ronald Reagan was charging into an election, soon to be granted a second term. Margaret Thatcher's second premiership was underway. The Canadian Prime Minister was the first Trudeau—though it might have been John Turner or Brian Mulroney.

Truman Capote died that year. Milan Kundera published *The Unbearable Lightness of Being*. Michael Jordan averaged 28 points per game and was named Rookie of the Year. The Tigers lost just five times in their first 40 games. They did not spend a single day out of first place and wound up winning

104 games. They swept the Royals in the American League Championship Series and dismantled the Padres in five games to win the World Series. The Doomsday Clock read three minutes 'til midnight.

Three and a half decades later I wake up most mornings and go on the internet to scan my newsfeed, to see whether the world has ended since last I checked. American democracy is currently under threat, peaceful demonstrations are labelled violent uprisings, armed men storm state houses, and law enforcement punishes citizens with impunity. A pandemic envelops the globe, killing hundreds of thousands of people.

Additionally, though no less existentially terrifying, the planet is in a spiral of warming and disjunction. We've reached a crucial moment in human history, and how we respond in a very short period of time will determine whether or not the Earth remains habitable beyond the current century.

In light of all of that, is anything short of total engagement appropriate? Is it purely solipsistic to participate in any pursuit not immediately concerned with social justice, carbon reduction, or advocating for the rights of others?

Gun violence rages. Populism is tilting stable nations toward authoritarianism. Xenophobia is on the rise. There are still Nazis—*literal Nazis*—pushing an agenda of fear and hatred. We're in the umpteenth week of Covid lockdown, and I'm dreaming of sitting in an Applebee's in suburban Syracuse watching Sox-Yanks, sitting at the bar drinking watery domestic beer, happy as a clam. This can't be right. I'm reading in bed, emotionally invested in Jane Leavy's account of Sandy Koufax's perfect game. I get mad about the prospect of expanding oil and gas extraction; I get just as upset when I worry about where the Blue Jays are going to dig up some pitching for next year.

Am I living with my head in the sand? Possibly. Probably. But also, there's this: Every baseball game you've ever attended or watched on TV or distractedly monitored via push notifications has taken place under the threat of nuclear annihilation. Every book you've read. Every new lover you've taken.

When Little Boy was dropped on Hiroshima, the Cubs led the National League by five-and-a-half games over the Cardinals. By the time Fat Man hit Nagasaki, the Cards had narrowed the gap by a half-game.

Consider that the A's won three straight Series while Vietnam seethed. Ty Cobb hit .401 the year *The Waste Land* was published.

The myth of lost innocence is as pervasive as it is fantastical. In reality, the present has always been fraught, the future perpetually in question, the past ever murky and ill-understood.

A pastime is a useful weapon to combat the sense of powerlessness that such calamity breeds. To check in regularly—even daily—to a place where the stakes are mostly imagined, or at least short of life or death, is to salvage one's sanity. Baseball can, amid the churn, provide stillness.

It's at least partially true that I'm performing moral contortions to justify this thing I do not wish to let go, this thing which has adhered to me since my earliest memories, this game which has delivered to me so much uncomplicated joy. But I'm distrustful of pitting engagement in opposition to entertainment. We can fight for the world while still enjoying it. Our efforts can sit alongside those things that make it worth saving. March on Washington in the afternoon, then catch the Nats and Phils as the sun cools and the moon rises over the Capitol. Max Scherzer striking out ten while you sit with a beer and a pretzel in your shirtsleeves is the perfect reminder of what it is we're struggling to preserve, because without the things that express and define our humanity—and baseball certainly fits that bill—we're not living, and not making much of a case for saving our civilization.

At the end of East 45th Street, Greta Thunberg stood before world leaders at the UN General Assembly and said, "You are failing us." Up in the Bronx, the Yankees had just won their 102nd game of the season to enjoy a nine-and-a-half game cushion over the Rays.

There are human endeavours that inoculate us against the horrors of existence. When announcing his decision to step down from his role as Chairman of the MacDowell Colony, the novelist Michael Chabon said, "[t]hese feel like such dire times, times of violence and dislocation, schism, paranoia, and the earth-scorching politics of fear. Babies have iPads, the ice caps are melting, and your smart refrigerator is eavesdropping on your lovemaking..." But, he said, "art makes the whole depressing thing more bearable." Agreed, I thought, but I'd add baseball to round out the sentiment. Or maybe I'd call baseball art.

I understand that the contemporary game is not without its problems, and yet when I see its perfect motion, the expressions of the faultless geometry at its heart, I forgive all of that. I see the game's power to enmesh us within a community, to encourage productive entanglements, putting us side by side in a grandstand both literal and figurative. I see our kids with the names of our towns across the front of their jerseys and T-shirts. I see us all situated in the warp of history, buoyed by the transparency of the simplest, starkest arrangement in sport: a pitcher and a batter. I see its offer of daily rescue for six months of the year from this increasingly Stygian reality.

There is also a part of this love for the game that resists all logic, evades all questioning, and defies all good sense. Present it as a heat map of the heart—cool blue on the corners, glowing red right down the middle. When asked to locate the animus of his passion for the game, Theo, one of my twin sons, at the time nine years old, could say only, "It's awesome!" Where eloquence fails, enthusiasm steps in.

It's the comfort of a place you can identify by the particular way the light falls on its recesses and angles, its green grass and white lines during evenings in April, in July, on afternoons in September. It's sunlight sweetened and enriched until it reaches a kind of golden crescendo before disappearing as the leaves begin to turn, because the team has turned in another lost campaign. But *that light*. You'd know it anywhere, and you tune in some days just to witness it.

It's Keith Jackson ("Whoooaaaaa, Nellie!") in a yellow blazer, calling *Monday Night Baseball*, introducing a clip of a dyspeptic manager—Earl Weaver or Billy Martin or Bobby Cox—getting ejected from a game. It's the memory of all that, or the YouTube-preserved video of it called up on a winter morning, to remind yourself that spring will eventually arrive.

It's Frank Robinson's smile and Eddie Murray's scowl. It's Howard Cosell calling Pete Rose "a gritty little guy with the skills that aren't quite what [a] superstar's are supposed to be."

It's a true doubleheader. Friday afternoons at Wrigley. A timely double play. It's Ichiro.

It's a night game at Tiger Stadium, amid the onset of football weather, the lights burning, visible even from across the river in Windsor. It's Goose Gossage refusing to intentionally walk Kirk Gibson, and then Gibson launching Gossage's 1–0 pitch into the second deck. It's Ernie Harwell conveying all that to you, a voice on air, drifting through the dark, making the night feel incrementally smaller, if only for those hours.

Christie and I returned to Detroit in 2019, this time with our three kids in tow. The Tigers were sweating through another hundred-loss campaign, waiting for their most recent glory days, personified by Miguel Cabrera, to age out, and for the near future to come into being. We stayed at the Book Cadillac Hotel in a beautiful room with a view straight up Shelby Street of the enormous Canadian flag flying on Windsor's waterfront. The hotel is a snapshot of Detroit's waxing and waning fortunes over the last century or so: when the inn opened in 1924 it was the tallest hotel in the world. In 1984, unprofitable and badly in need of updating, it closed for renovations, remaining shuttered for twenty-four years, empty and rotting. Right around the time they levelled the last of Tiger Stadium, the hotel reopened under the Westin banner, sporting new amenities but having discarded many of its most luxurious details.

In May 1939, it was in the Book Cadillac that Lou Gehrig, having played in 2,130 consecutive games dating back to June of 1925, but already suffering from the disease that would come to bear his name, collapsed on the hotel's grand staircase. He later met with Joe McCarthy, his Yankee manager, to tell him he couldn't play that day against the Tigers. You have to use your imagination to picture that scene now: the grand staircase is gone and the new lobby features a Starbucks.

We had a good time in the Motor City, which bore in its downtown all the symptoms of gentrification. It had become a little less Sarajevo, a little more Brooklyn: busy, creative, colourful, and more expensive. We ate Coney dogs and visited the Institute of Art, sat in a park and listened to a band work through Motown hits, and stood admiring Edward Dwight's riverside sculpture commemorating the Underground Railroad.

The Tigers weren't home that particular weekend, though we walked by their empty ballpark anyway, stood outside the gates and took photos of the tiger statues, and the statue of Harwell. Then I took the kids down to Michigan and Trumbull, where Tiger Stadium had been. In place of the old building there stands The Corner Ballpark, where the Detroit Police Athletic League hosts baseball, softball, and T-ball for local kids. We strode through the open gates and sat at a picnic table immediately behind the screen. It was a beautiful sunny Sunday morning in August. Two teams occupied the turf, one in blue T-shirts, one in yellow, along with a healthy cadre of volunteers, coaches, parents. The players were young—six or eight years old. They wore grey baseball pants, and most of them had socks pulled midway up the shin. Some in cleats, others in basketball shoes. They hit balls along the green turf. Their throws bounced or sailed wide of their intended targets. They laughed and shouted.

In the distance, dead centre and just shy of 440 feet from home plate, rose Tiger Stadium's old in-play flagpole. They'd intended to move it to the new ballpark, but wound up leaving it on the original spot and erecting a new one downtown. So the old one stands yet, resolute amid the wild galloping horses of progress, a monument to neglect or stubbornness, I'm not sure which, or if it couldn't be both.

# A HANDFUL OF DIRT

Each March, Japanese high school teams play the Spring Koshien near Kobe, just as we here in North America are settling in for the opening of another big league season. The Koshien tournament is equivalent in scale to March Madness, and filled with just as much emotion and drama. It's the first of two annual tournaments; the Spring Koshien kicks off a season of ball that culminates with August's Summer Koshien, the larger of the two. In each, dozens of teams from across Japan play instant-elimination games in front of crowds of nearly fifty thousand at Koshien Stadium. Millions more watch on TV, and the pressure is impressive. Win or lose, most participants end the tournament in tears.

If you can locate a reliable streaming feed, you'll see boys in brilliant white uniforms play conservative, fundamentally sound baseball, as near to aesthetic perfection as you can imagine, the sole blemish provided by the telltale ping of aluminum bats. The pageant is opulent: players stand outside their dugouts before the first pitch and then sprint en masse toward the plate, where they meet in the batter's box, standing in straight, opposing lines. They bow to one another and to the day's umpires before sprinting to their positions. The first pitch is heralded by an air raid siren. Fans dressed in school colours sing, play brass instruments, and cheer through small bullhorns.

Since 1915, most of Japan's elite baseball players have seen action in the Koshien, including home run king Sadaharu Oh, one-time Yankees slugger Hideki Matsui, Angels designated hitter/pitcher Shohei Ohtani, and Ichiro Suzuki, who played in the Koshien in 1991, primarily as a pitcher, though he did manage to hit .505 for his three-year high school career. His efforts, though impressive, were not sufficient to help his school, Aikodai Meiden, emerge victorious from the

Koshien's imposing gauntlet. As consolation, he was drafted by the Pacific League's Orix BlueWave, for whom he went on to rack up 1,278 base hits, becoming a superstar of Michael Jordan-like stature in Japan.

When I set about writing this book, Ichiro was about to begin his thirteenth season with the Seattle Mariners, albeit after an interruption of seven campaigns spent with the New York Yankees and Miami Marlins. He arrived at camp in the spring of 2018 after a winter of contract uncertainty that very nearly saw him without a Major League team. He was reportedly mulling the possibility of returning to Japan when a slew of injuries to the Mariners' corps of everyday outfielders thrust him into the arms of his old team.

He returned to Safeco Field in March dressed in the home team's uniform for the first time since the first Obama administration, and he did so not as an All-Star right fielder and on-base threat, but as a left fielder called upon only out of necessity. His reintroduction to the Seattle faithful was warm and emotional—precisely the sort of circumstance that prompts fans to spend princely sums on souvenirs. Even the least cynical among us was forced to consider the likelihood that merchandising opportunities informed the decision-making process; there were other younger outfielders among the field of free agents when the Mariners committed to bringing Ichiro back to the Pacific Northwest.

Ichiro was forty-four years old at the time, which is paleolithic in baseball terms. White Sox legend Minnie Miñoso collected one base hit at fifty. Charley O'Leary was either fifty-one or fifty-eight (uncertainty and debate hover over his actual birthdate) when he pinch-hit for the St. Louis Browns in 1934. Satchel Paige pitched at fifty-nine. The thread common to all of those feats is that they were publicity stunts engineered by some of the greatest hucksters in the history of both baseball and capitalist enterprise. Neither O'Leary nor Miñoso were viable everyday ballplayers by the time they took their last cuts

(Satch was another story, a man who did seem to have found a way to cheat time). With his return Ichiro, meanwhile, aimed to provide quality at-bats and adequate defence for a team that hoped to contend for a Wild Card berth. The average age of a ballplayer in 2020 was about twenty-eight, and the stark fact is that the list of players who've proven effective in their forties (to say nothing of their fifties) is a very short one, and it's heavy on pitchers—junkballers, mostly, and masters of the knuckleball, a pitch that places roughly as much strain on the body as a game of catch with a six-year-old.

But then, there have been so few like Ichiro, who began his grueling, year-round training regimen in the third grade, throwing, swinging, exercising, and working out every day. He claimed to have only taken a few days off thereafter during his entire lengthy career, and hated doing so. The precision, order, and ritual with which he approached the game allowed him to maintain well into the twilight of his career the same litheness he possessed when he first took the mound at Koshien Stadium.

That regime, and his firm and extreme habits, made him the object of both wonder and derision when he arrived in America in the spring of 2001. He didn't look the part of a ballplayer, at least not the classically American variety, which led many to suggest he wouldn't be able to play the game here. He showed immediately that he could, and brilliantly— he was named both Rookie of the Year and the American League's Most Valuable Player, though he did so in a way that was thrillingly different from previous award winners.

What made Ichiro such a compelling ballplayer is precisely what makes watching the Spring Koshien so entrancing. It's baseball, unquestionably, but baseball filtered through a completely unique set of experiences. Inherent in the excitement of a tournament like Koshien is the poignancy of the possibility that the young players, once eliminated from the contest, will never again know the terror and joy of playing on that old stadium's signature all-dirt infield and felt-green outfield. Similarly, at the end of Ichiro's MLB career there was an added frisson to everything he did on the field, because he was doing it after his fortieth birthday, in the face of time's relentless advancement. Notwithstanding the man's insistence that he'd like to play until he was *at least* fifty years old, there was the distinct possibility that every achievement—each putout, each base hit—could very well be his last.

There's a tradition at Koshien that, at the end of each game, the eliminated teams' players stoop to the ground and gather a handful of infield dirt, and carry it away in a bag, or a jar, or in the pockets of their uniform pants. *I was there*, the treasured soil attests in later years. *Whatever came after in life, I played there, and I knew the glory*. Ichiro did not bend to the temptation of such nostalgia at any point in his career, in Japan or America, but that didn't stop those of us in the cheap seats, or watching from home, from latching onto such mementos.

I didn't want to write a second book about baseball. My first was more successful than I expected it would be, and I knew that producing another would please some people, not the least of whom was my publisher. But I resisted. There were a lot of personal reasons for that, and the biggest areas of concern for me were, first, that the sequel is rarely as good as the original and, second, that I wanted to be known as something more than a baseball writer (despite the fact that many of my favourite writers, whose work has taught me much about the world beyond baseball, were "just" baseball writers).

But then Ichiro re-signed with the Seattle Mariners, a homecoming of sorts that I wanted to chronicle. Just months into his second tour with the M's, though, his waning abilities were apparent. When, in May of 2018, he bowed to reality and stepped away from playing, in what would prove a segue to his eventual retirement ten months later, I lost all my reservations; I needed urgently to write about Ichiro while it was all still fresh.

What followed was immersion and reflection. I knew Ichiro was my favourite player, and had been for almost two decades. What wasn't immediately clear to me was why that was true. I hadn't ever forced myself to perform that kind of inventory, hadn't asked what elevated him from being one of those players I admire, like Fred McGriff or Bo Bichette, to a person who seemed to constitute some element of my self-identity.

Writing about Ichiro also required looking more closely at him than I ever had before, and what I repeatedly encountered was a person who resisted my understanding. He's a supremely enigmatic figure, and though very real linguistic and cultural factors lie between us, I don't think those are the true barriers to my comprehension. Much of his persona is constructed in ways seemingly designed to refract attention, to send scrutiny prismatically off in other directions. What the Ichiro scholar is left with, in their attempts to nibble at the borders of The Question of Ichiro, is a void surrounded by a tight circle of ancillary and adjacent knowledge: the historical antecedents to his style of play, the elements of Japanese baseball that informed his game, the teams he played for, the times he played in, and the specific and personal reasons for their own interest in him. A handful of dirt.

For most Koshien participants, there is no professional baseball in their future. They are not drafted to the NPB, and they do not make the leap across the ocean to play in America. The attention and glory they know in that big old stadium is experienced once. Their days after that moment of kneeling to collect the infield dirt may echo down thereafter. How does someone make sense of an experience so big? The most resonant physical residue is a vase or a bag or a small ornamental box of dirt placed on a shelf, there to be stared at over and over again. Beyond the simple claim of presence—whether as witness or participant—what more can be gleaned from such an artifact?

It's possible to look at something for half your life and not completely understand it. Maybe that's part of the appeal. It's probably the reason a person *keeps* looking, even as the object of attention refuses to offer up anything more in the way of knowing. Puzzle over it a little longer and the relationship between the familiar and foreign may begin to grow indistinct, until it finally registers as the birth of something new.

# THE GLOVE GOES ON THE HAND
## YOU DON'T THROW WITH

It was nine on a Saturday morning in early summer, and I was sitting on the unyielding wooden bleachers of Chemung Lake District Lions Club Park, a lazy fly ball north of Peterborough, Ontario. A windless day, the heat rising and prickly. There wasn't much shade to be found, and I spared a thought for those parents who'd be watching the game scheduled for eleven, when the sun's intensity would transition from welcome to murderous.

"She'll be a hot one," said one parent, a sandal on the bleacher row in front of him, a Tim Hortons coffee cup in his hand. The coaches—a collection of well-meaning volunteers ready to attempt to orchestrate the chaotic movement of children around the crushed gravel infield of a softball diamond—all carried Tim's cups too. "I feel like I'm being cooked from the inside," said one coach, but kept sipping just the same.

My twin boys, Theo and Cormac, were six years old and eager to play T-ball, because I'd told them again and again that was where they'd learn the rudiments of baseball, a game in which they'd both expressed an interest. Though at that point they were probably only acting out of filial loyalty, because then as now, roughly a third of what came out of my mouth on a given day from April through October, was about baseball. I was passing my obsession on to them, as well as to Adelaide, our first-born, who was then ten. Or I was trying to, anyway.

The boys and their teammates were dressed in the red T-shirts that comprised their uniforms. Accordingly, they'd been christened the Red Sox, though just about all of them also wore Blue Jays caps. That Saturday morning they were playing the Orange Sluggers, several of whom were draped in T-shirts that reached down to their ankles. The whole unruly knot of them—Red Sox and Sluggers alike—stood on the infield, led through warm-ups by the same volunteers who had painted the lines on the diamond and erected the tee at home plate. It takes a village.

Those registered for Lions Club T-ball were between the ages of four and eight, so the teams encompassed a wide sampling of ability, from those who'd already discovered a bit of physical power and grace to those yet to assume captaincy of their limbs. My boys were average specimens, athletically speaking, but if they actually caught a ball thrown their way it was cause for great celebration, for them and for me. They would take their whacks and run the bases, advancing one base at a time to allow everyone their chance. This was T-ball, and it was really about breeding familiarity with gloves and balls, bats and bases. Nobody would hit a ball as far as the outfield grass. The fielders would stand in clumps around the bases, so that there were two or three first basemen, two or three shortstops, and so on. Very few balls would be caught. They would play just three innings or until the hour was up, whichever came first. During that span kids would run the wrong way, they'd run home right after touching first base, they'd turn to face the backstop when they batted, they would mix up their top and bottom hands, tangling their arms as they attempted to swing, weakly clubbing the tee instead of the ball perched thereon, which would dribble off and settle in the dust in front of the plate. The volunteer standing nearby would have to decide whether or not to consider it a hit, and if he did, he'd coax the child to run toward first, sometimes taking her or him by the hand to guide them down the line.

There was a persistent and unfortunate tug in me toward the idea of how baseball should be played. I wanted to call out to my boys, "Stand there!" "Run that way!" "Catch the ball!" Mostly I tamped down that urge, though I did allow myself one outburst, when both boys, standing near first base, removed their gloves and slid them over their right hands. "Boys," I called by way of reminder, "the glove goes on the hand you *don't* throw with!" They waved and smiled and switched hands, though it wouldn't matter when the ball next came their way; it'd sail by just the same.

The heat was downright obnoxious by the second inning, and word had spread through the Red Sox that the bases made excellent places to rest, like small sofa cushions; a kid sat on first base with his glove on his head, a girl squatted on second, and two kids shared third, including Theo. It required a conscious effort on my part not to call out and direct my kids. If I really assessed the situation, could I blame him? Could I blame any of them?

When the hour was up, the handshakes given, and no final score counted, my boys came to meet me in the bleachers. They were happy as songbirds. Theo estimated that the Red Sox scored 18 runs, and he wanted to know the record for the most runs tallied by a team in a big league game. "I think you guys came close," I told him. Cormac wanted to go to the nearby playground instead of talking ball. Teammates climbed into vans and cars and trucks with parents and siblings as the next game got underway, the little sets of bleachers still full of parents, some of whom were trying to coach from the stands, while others succeeded in keeping their comments to a few encouraging cries.

As we drove home with the windows down, I realized that lessons were indeed being learned at the ball field, though they weren't all the intended ones, like how to catch and throw, and the proper order in which to run the bases, and they weren't exclusively being learned by the intended pupils. The biggest lesson, in fact, was being learned by the hard-headed parents, myself included, and it was a tough one, though maybe we'd get there yet.

# SNAP, GO, FLING

When America closes its eyes and tries to imagine "America," it pictures something like Grand Haven, Michigan: earnest, polished, with one foot in a past characterized by neon diner decor, and one foot firmly in a present consisting of abundant craft beer and wireless internet. Freshly painted fences sit alongside ghost signage on old brick walls. Beach parking is free.

We'd arrived in Grand Haven from the Upper Peninsula, which offered beauty embarrassing in its abundance. We lay on our backs on a stretch of Superior shore and watched the Perseids pour their space junk over an incredible sky. We swam in the icy water of the world's largest freshwater lake, small beneath pink, violet, and gold clouds embroidering an already extravagant sunset. White pine, yellow birch, and red maple perched atop the tall bluffs behind us.

But the U.P. has no minor-league baseball, and you can't call it summer without minor-league ball, so we made our way next across the Straits of Mackinac to the mitten. En route we drove through any number of former towns that underscore, as proud Midwesterner Hanif Abdurraqib has written, "the difference between a place that *is* closed, and a place that *has* closed." Great tracts of the state, away from the beaches and the national parks and the suburban business campuses, were falling into ruin.

Traverse City's a tourist town, though, and seemed to be doing just fine. They host a team in the Northwoods League called the Pit Spitters. The Northwoods League is a wood-bat league, not affiliated with Major League Baseball. In this way it differs from the typical minor league of your imagination; these players are not about to be called up to the big club. Instead, they're college players on summer furlough, using their time to get experience with wooden bats and grass fields (in NCAA games they swing metal and play on plastic). These kids spend the hot months playing a short season in the hopes that the experience will make them more attractive to Major League teams. The NWL has teams dotting the Midwest— Minnesota, Wisconsin, Illinois, and all the way up to Thunder Bay, Ontario. As for the Spitters' nickname, northern Michigan is, they'll have you know, the tart cherry-growing capital of the United States.

The name is local and quirky, but the charm evaporates a little when you consider the Spitters' name and logos were crafted by the same San Diego-based design firm that concocted the brand identities of the Amarillo Sod Poodles, the Lehigh Valley IronPigs, the Rocket City Trash Pandas, the Richmond Flying Squirrels, and the Akron RubberDucks. This, like most apparently carefree things you happen upon these days, is a carefully curated experience.

Our seats at Pit Spitters Park were right behind the dugout on the third base side. It was two-dollar hot dog night *and* two-dollar beer night. The queues were long. The Pit Spitters' starting pitcher was a skinny kid with long hair and longer limbs. His pants flapped above his ankles, as though he'd experienced a growth spurt since being fitted for his uniform, which very well might have been the case. The night was lovely and cool, and the sky surrendered its colour slowly. The home team jumped out early and scored often.

Cherry and strawberry seasons had passed; the apples were reddening. Only a few games remained. A Pit Spitter lay down a bunt and the runner on third crashed in: a perfect suicide squeeze. Cheers rose and then diminished. The lanky pitcher twirled a gem. The Spitters blanked the Rockford Rivets 8–0, and we drove out of Traverse City past darkened fields.

In Grand Rapids a week later, we sat on the first base side a dozen rows up as the West Michigan Whitecaps took on the Great Lakes Loons in a ballpark named for a bank. The Whitecaps, then managed by former Tiger Lance Parrish, are a Detroit affiliate in the Low-A Midwest League, which means their job is to sand the rough edges off twenty-year-old prospects in order to advance them higher up the chain.

Whitman saw in baseball "the snap, go, fling, of the American atmosphere," and we bought tickets up the first base side so that we could ingest that energy. We found it on the field, yes, but also in the attendant hucksterism and commerce, our placement not as fanatics but as customers, targets of a stultifying corporate control made insidious for being nearly undetectable. It was the homogeneity that ultimately gave it away, the sense that all corners had been rounded and the cumbersome aspects of the experience had been focus-grouped out of existence. Quirks existed only insofar as patrons had indicated they approved of certain idiosyncrasies to give them some thorn upon which to hang this feeling of being alive and present, this moment, taking photos and posting them to social media. The hashtags were provided for you on the videoboard: remember to like and follow.

For the sake of pleasure, though, we suspended our cynicism and, quite literally, bought in. The Whitecaps defeated the Loons 5–1, and the kids were thrilled with the free duffle bags we'd been given, sponsored by a local energy provider, and the hats we picked up in the spacious gift shop. I am happiest with the memory of the organist situated on the concourse, just behind home plate, and I marvel at her ability to fill out her scorecard between musical flourishes. How did she keep it all straight? My scorecard was unfinished; I'd total the pitching lines the next day over coffee.

In the morning, back in Grand Haven, we stopped into Hostetter's News Agency at the corner of Washington and 2nd. The place was a jumble. Immediately inside the door, a TV blared an episode of *Columbo* at near full volume. The woman behind the counter greeted us in a flat, shouty tone. She was eighty if she was a day. There was a shelf behind her head with pornography on it—on VHS. An aisle of magazines, a full shelf of puzzle books. Faded postcards. Candy that had partially melted or gone brittle with age. In the back, a selection of cigars, jars of pipe tobacco, exotic cigarettes. For twenty dollars, you could have a copy of the *Tribune*, wrapped in plastic, from the day after the White Sox won the 2005 World Series. On a rack hidden in a strange warren in the middle of the store, I stumbled onto unopened packs of baseball cards from when I was a pre-teen, about Adelaide's age, and I smiled with delight. They were priced with a marker: a buck sixty-five. I bought a handful. We also picked up a *New Yorker* and a Sudoku book and some Tootsie Rolls, and then we headed to the beach.

We sat motionless beneath flapping umbrellas. I opened the first pack of cards and Ken Griffey Jr. stared up at me. The sky was blue overhead but dark to the west of us. Rain paraded in visible bands off Wisconsin and passed across the lake, made landfall north of us and moved on. The sun burned back through the cloud cover, and the horizon appeared to lift up into the sky's white phosphorescence. On the card, Griffey was following through, bat flung out behind him, probably sending a double bounding off the Kingdome's blue wall. The yellow S on his batting helmet was brilliant, and the white of his uniform crisp, bright, and impossibly beautiful.

# A PHOTOGRAPH OF GAYLORD PERRY BEING INVESTIGATED FOR FOREIGN SUBSTANCES

Gaylord Perry toiled for twenty-two seasons in the majors, and the look on his face suggests it was hard toil indeed. Wind worn, exasperated, he mutely submits to yet another examination of his cap, his head, his uniform, for a dab of Vaseline, a smear of K-Y. It might or might not have been there—Perry's success rested on the twin pillars of a doctored ball's unpredictability, and the thought, instilled in the head of each batter he faced, that the ball *might* be materially abetted in its tortuous journey from mound to plate.

This scene, captured mid-investigation, is from somewhere between 1972 and '75, after he and Frank Duffy were traded by the Giants to Cleveland for Sudden Sam McDowell. We don't know where the game takes place (the photo's greyscale presentation makes it hard to say if Perry's uniform is home white or road grey), or precisely when, but we can assert with confidence that the umpire failed to uncover irrefutable evidence of malfeasance; the righty wouldn't be ejected from a contest for such an offence until late August 1982, his twenty-first season. For that infraction, the American League suspended him ten games and levied a $250 fine.

Not that there wasn't reason for suspicion on the part of the ump. At that point in his career, Perry had either recently or was soon to publish *Me and the Spitter: An Autobiographical Confession*, confirming in print what everyone had known for a decade or more.

Perry broke in with the Giants in 1962, and remained in San Francisco through the '71 season, but his initial point of contact with the dark art of the spitball probably came in 1964 when he shared the clubhouse with Bob Shaw. Shaw was a right-handed journeyman who kicked around the league, garnered some Cy Young votes with the White Sox in '59, then had an All-Star year in '62 for Milwaukee, but by the time he landed in San Fran he'd become the sort of fungible presence in a bullpen sometimes known as a "warm body."

You can imagine them out there, can't you, between Perry's starts, discussing the finer points of deception, the student and his mentor, all those hours to kill in the bullpen at Candlestick Park, with the cold brine and petrochemical tang of the Bay swirling about them. You get a tube of K-Y Jelly, Shaw would have counselled, and you put a dollop in your hair, on your hat, inside the neck of the jersey, the cuff of your right pant leg. "Load it up in about three different places," he would later tell a reporter, "so you don't go to the same place."

Credit Perry here for recognizing the lay of the land. He was playing baseball, not seeking ordination. So Perry fell into the herky improvisational rhythm of American professional life, reasoning, we might surmise, that the only fault in cheating is when it's done artlessly.

Perry would run his fingers "across the underside of the bill of that cap, down the right side of his face," as Dave Niehaus would suggestively narrate while doing the play-by-play during Perry's early-eighties stint in Seattle. The mystery pitch, it was sometimes called, a euphemistic bit of doublespeak among the initiated. But everybody knew what it was.

Perry could throw just about anything. He had a forkball, as well as a decent fastball, and could harass batters with a 12-to-6 humpback curveball, but it was the mystery pitch that made the rest of them more effective, dancing and dipping toward home, scrambling a hitter's eye, shaking his confidence.

"Slider," the radio and TV announcers would say, "or could have been a changeup."

"The wet one," Gaylord's older brother Jim sometimes called it.

By the time the photo was taken, Perry was halfway through a two-decade career, but he already looks ancient. In San Francisco he kept things pretty trim, or so suggests the photographic record, but once he moved on from the Giants he seems to have achieved a more or less permanent state of dishevelment. Sign of the times, perhaps, or sign of the man's growing comfort with his place in the world. He prevailed in an era that's hard for us to parse now, at this remove. It's too easy to call his appearance avuncular—somebody's pack-a-day uncle, Oldsmobile and wingtips and dirty jokes, taking slugs of Wild Turkey from a tin flask. But what he really looks like is a father. As a child I'd have looked at him and thought, yes, this is what a man of a certain vintage looks like, coming as he did from a generation of men who looked older than we do now, even at the same age. My father's peers were naval officers, but they too belonged to this aftershave-rich, golf-spiked branch of humanity.

Perry was a pro ballplayer, but not someone you'd call an athlete. He looks, in the photo, as in most photos, like a man who grunts huffily when he bends over to tie his shoes.

The second figure, the umpire with the bill of Perry's cap in his hand, deserves some scrutiny, too. I can't identify him by the back of his head, this employee of the American League, but I know that, on that mound, on that field, in whichever ballpark in whatever junior circuit city, he's the law.

I'm not sure if Perry is our hero or antihero in this scenario, but either way we're rooting against the umpire. At least I am. In the reductionist Manichean reading of this text, the ump's a functionary, a heavy, there to stand in for whatever machine you care to picture: the state, the system, the generation ahead of yours. His job is to harsh Perry's vibe.

With not a little simmering animosity, Perry submits to the inspection, this routine indignity performed by our mystery ump, without conviction but with the practised wiliness and cynicism of a person tasked with arbitrating the daily spike-and-dirt struggle of men paid to outhustle one another. Perry, I have no doubt, shrugged this off, bulldogging his way through, as was his custom.

Time shifts social mores. The spitball was once legal. Then it wasn't. What trick or tool did they take away from hitters? That's what Perry might argue. In order to even things out a bit, it can be necessary to fudge the lines, to work outside the margins. Use what you've got. And it worked: 314 wins, a Cy Young Award in each league, a plaque in the Hall of Fame. He carved a hard, hoary career out of the murky zone between culpability and deniability.

Is the secret sauce there? Yeah, it's probably there, though concealed enough to make it hard for the ump to say with any certainty that it's there. Sometimes Perry would put something on his zipper, because no ump wanted to go poking around there.

Why did Gaylord Perry go to such lengths? Did his success depend on the spitball? Maybe, and maybe not. I suspect, though, that the foreign substance's presence on all those different uniforms and caps—eight different teams in two leagues, from Kennedy to Reagan, *Please Please Me* to *Thriller*—proves that he did depend on it, that Gaylord Perry was not Gaylord Perry if not doing what Gaylord Perry did. A person does not come lightly to such a decision, but rather only after performing some deep and expurgatory self-analysis. This is who I am, a person might eventually conclude, and I'm going to ride this horse until we both expire.

Rob Dibble was once a member of the Cincinnati Reds' dominating relief pitching corps dubbed the "Nasty Boys," whose collective professional zenith came in 1990, when they were instrumental in helping the Reds sweep Oakland in the World Series. Twice an All-Star, Dibble had a rocket for a right arm and a short-fuse temper. The rocket burned quickly and then flared out; he pitched his last big-league inning for Milwaukee in 1995. Thereafter Dibble reinvented himself as a broadcaster and purveyor of fiery hot takes, where that short fuse often landed him in trouble, or out of a job. In the spring of 2001 he was in the employ of ESPN and he found occasion to opine that Ichiro—then in his first spring training with the Mariners—would not find great success in Major League Baseball. So confident was Dibble that Ichiro would not win the batting title that he pledged to streak through Times Square with Ichiro's number 51 tattooed on his hindquarters should Ichiro earn the distinction.

Ichiro, of course, had a pretty decent season in 2001, making an All-Star appearance and winning the Rookie of the Year award and the AL MVP trophy. He led the league in stolen bases (56) and base hits (242). He was given a Gold Glove for defensive excellence and a Silver Slugger Award as one of the league's three best-hitting outfielders. He also won the batting title with a .350 average.

There's satisfaction in knowing that the debt was eventually owed. Dibble had expressed, however gaseously, what was a popular sentiment: by virtue of its differences, Japanese baseball was not capable of producing a star-calibre Major League hitter. Among the list of knocks against Japanese baseball are that the parks are smaller, the ball is smaller and lighter, the season is shorter (143 games versus 162). There are also, as you might imagine, a host of other "reasons," which range from vague preference to outright xenophobia. Beneath all of them lies the bedrock objection: it just isn't the American game.

Which is absolutely correct. It's the Japanese game, adapted from the American game as it was introduced to Tokyo in about 1872. In the early twentieth century it thrived as an amateur sport, popular among high schools and universities. A sixty thousand seat stadium opened in 1924 to accommodate the aforementioned wildly popular high school tournament; the stadium (modified several times, and now with a somewhat reduced capacity) still hosts its namesake competition. By the 1930s there was such a mania for baseball in Japan that a tour of high-wattage US stars was organized, including Ruth, Gehrig, and Jimmie Foxx. Shortly thereafter, the first Japanese professional league began operating. After the Second World War necessitated an interruption to the 1945 season, the Japan Baseball League was back to playing a full schedule in 1946, and before the 1950 season had reorganized itself into Nippon Professional Baseball, comprised of the Central and Pacific leagues. It operates to this day, and as of 2020, of the sixty-one Japanese players to have competed in Major League Baseball, only four did not first play in NPB.

The first Japanese-born ballplayer in the Majors was a six-foot lefthander named Masanori Murakami. The Nankai Hawks sent him and two other prospects to the US to train with the San Francisco Giants in the spring of 1964 in what both organizations hoped would prove to be a regular and mutually beneficial arrangement. From training camp, the Giants assigned Murakami to their minor league club in Fresno, where he pitched well enough to earn a late-season call-up to the Giants. He made his big league debut at Shea Stadium on September 1, facing four Mets, striking out two of them, giving up a base hit, and inducing a groundball to end his inning of relief. He went on to appear in eight more games that season, pitching to an ERA of 1.80. Pleased with those results, the Giants offered Murakami a contract for '65, which he signed. Once home in

Japan for the offseason, though, he faced pressure from family as well as the Hawks to return for good. It had apparently never occurred to Nankai GM Makoto Tachibana that the Hawks' erstwhile young lefty would perform well enough in America for any of this to become an issue. Dismissive of San Francisco's legal standing, the Hawks signed Murakami to a contract of their own for the 1965 season.

Much wrangling ensued, with both sides aware that they were fighting not only for the services of Masanori Murakami but for precedent in all future trans-Pacific baseball dealings. An uneasy compromise was eventually struck that allowed for Murakami to honour his '65 deal with the Giants before returning to Japan for good in 1966. He never again played in America, though he later did some post-retirement scouting for the Giants. The contentious nature of the exchange established mutual distrust between MLB and NPB, and thirty-one years passed before another Japanese player suited up in the Majors. To do so, pitcher Hideo Nomo exploited a loophole in the rules, retiring as a player with the Kintetsu Buffaloes in order to be granted international free agent status; he thereafter signed with the Los Angeles Dodgers. Nomo's experience with the labyrinthine rules governing such player movement led to the development of the international posting system in place today, whereby Japanese teams may elect to make a player available to MLB teams in exchange for a posting fee. Nomo's success with the Dodgers—he was the 1995 Rookie of the Year—increased demand. The exodus had begun.

Prior to Ichiro in 2001, however, only pitchers had made the trans-Pacific jump, which likely contributed to Dibble's doubts, and the misgivings of others, including Seattle manager Lou Piniella. In Ichiro's first spring training, the skipper noted that all Ichiro seemed capable of hitting was ground balls to the opposite field. He suggested the outfielder try pulling the ball, a suggestion Ichiro met by pulling a home run to right in his next Cactus League game.

Ichiro's doubters were further fed by noting that he had a body type more common among jockeys than sluggers. What became apparent, though, as that first summer warmed and then broke into its full floral display, was that Ichiro's skillset was perfectly suited to a style of play that exploited contemporary baseball's ample seams and pores. It was a style largely foreign to the homer-happy American game circa the turn of this century, and with it he found historic success.

In 2018, the latest big-name import from Japan was Shohei Ohtani. In five seasons with the NPB's Hokkaido Nippon-Ham Fighters, Ohtani was a three-time All-Star, an MVP, and a Japan Series champion. He won 42 games as a pitcher, struck out 624 batters, and threw the fastest pitch in NPB history. He also hit 48 home runs, primarily playing in the outfield or as designated hitter on days he wasn't pitching. He made the decision in 2017 to submit himself to the international posting process, and Major League teams, lured by the rare combination of pitching acumen and hitting power, made him their best offers. The Los Angeles Angels emerged the winners, and Ohtani arrived at their camp in Tempe, Arizona with a great deal of expectation piled atop his shoulders.

He did not initially fare well. By the close of camp, Ohtani had failed to prove himself as either a hitter or a hurler to the satisfaction of his critics. There was some question as to whether the Angels should send him to the minors for seasoning or, if that would constitute too great a humiliation for organization and player alike, keep him on the bench in the season's early days.

It was reminiscent of Ichiro's introduction in more ways than one, and in fact mirrored the experience of virtually every player who's attempted the transition from Japan to MLB. In each case, the player has been made to suffer an inordinate weight, to stand as a one-man plebiscite on the viability of Japanese baseball. The doubts are raised anew, the deficiencies reiterated, the odds of success considered low. It doesn't seem to matter that there's enough history to say that, though there have been some notable disappointments, Japanese players have proven their ability to make the transition to the American game.

Ohtani, it happened, was either slow to get his legs in spring training or was executing a beautiful con. The Angels elected to use their new player right out of the gate, and the dividends were immediate. Two weeks into the regular season he'd won both games he'd pitched, struck out 18 batters, taken a perfect game into the seventh inning, collected a base hit in his first at-bat—on the first pitch he saw—and doubled, tripled, and belted three home runs.

By the end of his first season in North America, Ohtani had knocked 22 homers, slugged .564 with a .285 average, and racked up 61 RBIs in 104 games. Before being shut down with a shoulder injury, he pitched 51 2/3 innings, struck out 63 batters, and went 4–2 with a 3.31 ERA.

His doubters were forced to concede the very real possibility that Ohtani, who is built less like a jockey and more like a slender granite column, could emerge as the greatest combined pitching-hitting threat since Babe Ruth a century earlier.

Beyond their divergent physical statures, there is an obvious point of departure between Ichiro and Ohtani. Where Ichiro had long worked to perfect the sort of incremental game—get 'em on, get 'em over, get 'em in—most often associated with Japanese baseball, Ohtani played the quintessential American game, one characterized by power: 98 mph fastballs and tape-measure home runs. Ohtani's continued success would serve to blur the line between the Japanese and American games, leaving critics with no more planks in their platform of doubt save the most obvious and base one.

Since Ichiro's debut two decades ago, the trickle has become a steady current, with position players including Hideki Matsui, Kazuo Matsui, Akinori Iwamura, Norichika Aoki, Munenori Kawasaki, Kosuke Fukudome, and Shogo Akiyama all making their mark in the majors. They joined pitchers like Ichiro's teammate-for-two-games Yusei Kikuchi, Kazuhiro Sasaki (already established as the Mariners' closer when Ichiro debuted), Yu Darvish, Masahiro Tanaka, Kenta Maeda, Hiroki Kuroda, Tomokazu Ohka, Daisuke Matsuzaka, and about two dozen others. Broadening the geographic scope to a continental scale, Asian-born players—totally unrepresented in MLB thirty years ago and exceedingly rare at the time of Ichiro's debut—have assumed a place in virtually every big-league clubhouse. Players from South Korea include Chan Ho Park (the first Korean representative in MLB, debuting in 1994), Seunghwan Oh, Ji-Man Choi, Shin-Soo Choo, Hyun Jin Ryu, and Hee-Seop Choi. Taiwan has produced sixteen big leaguers, including Chien-Ming Wang, Wei-Yin Chen, and Wei-Chung Wang. It seems likely, too, based on the growing popularity of the game in China, that a coming wave of Chinese players is not far off.

Ichiro was a test balloon, probing the viability. Decades of established baseball wisdom stated that the Japanese game—and Asian baseball, by extension—was of such inferior quality that it could not produce hitters capable of becoming every-day contributors in North America. This belief coupled nativist pride and racial pigeonholing. Pitchers—like the pioneers Murakami and Nomo—got something of a pass, presumably because there's room for guile, craft, and finesse—all core tenets of the Japanese game—in the art of pitching. But with almost no adjustment period, Ichiro began earning individual hardware while helping his team to more victories than any American League club before or since. Arguably, there's no Ohtani without Ichiro, or at least no Ohtani in an American clubhouse. Ichiro endured the doubts and beat them back by producing daily, yearly, and by the decade. He evinced stamina and endurance, dismantling the arguments of those who suggested, suggestively, that the Japanese "style of play" wasn't suited for America. And once underway, the movement from East to West became a microscale representation of twenty-first century hyper-global exchange. Ichiro brought to the American League a smaller version of baseball, related directly to the game played on domestic sporting grounds in lavish wooden baseball palaces a century earlier.

Such cross-pollination probably would have occurred with or without Ichiro's success, though if he'd failed to make a dent wearing a Mariners uniform it would have been delayed; by years or by decades, we'll never know. But presented with such indisputable proof of Asian players' worthiness, it was inevitable that the American baseball power structure, whose primary language is economically inflected, would begin to cast their talent-snaring nets toward Japan, and beyond.

# AMERICAN BERSERK

As the twentieth century narrowed toward the vise of the new millennium, a novel anxiety arose. It was likely nothing more than garden-variety pre-millennial angst—the nagging fear of bank accounts being wiped out and airplanes dropping from the sky at the stroke of midnight, Y2K—but it found strange expressions in the cultural sphere: survivalist cult narratives, an odd affinity for synthetic materials and artificiality, *The Matrix*. We were, quite consciously, preparing for a future we were sure was within reach, and we were hedging our bets as to whether that future would bring continued prosperity or global catastrophe.

Baseball wasn't immune. Still licking the wounds suffered during the 1994 players' strike, baseball—or the cadre of oligarchs and technocrats who control and steer it—seemed to sense that the game's implicit focus on history might put it out of the favour of a decidedly future-thinking populace. In the face of all that, the game got a little desperate.

Matters reached peak absurdity in 1998. On July 18, the Seattle Mariners staged Turn Ahead the Clock Night during a game against the Kansas City Royals at the UFO-like Kingdome, a strange promotion that claimed to present baseball as it might look in 2027: sleeveless pullover uniforms, logos oversized and askew, shiny silver cleats and gloves, and a DeLorean dispatched to transport the man set to throw the ceremonial first pitch. It was garish and disposable and fun, and Major League Baseball liked it so much they repeated the promotion the following season.

Of course 1998 was also the summer that America was captivated by moonshots and the chase for Roger Maris's single-season record of 61 homers. Bunyanesque St. Louis Cardinals first baseman Mark McGwire and Chicago Cubs outfielder Sammy Sosa raced to see who would be the first to best Maris's mark. McGwire, large and solid as an oak, had four home runs through his first four games and was off to the races. Sosa—whippet-lean when he debuted with the Rangers in 1989 before being flipped to the White Sox the same year, then dealt to the Cubs, and by '98 equally as brawny as McGwire—got off to a slow start but closed the gap by clearing the fence twenty times in the month of June. By mid-August the sluggers were tied at 47, and media coverage went from heated to breathless. McGwire eventually won the race, hitting his 62nd on September 8 and finishing the campaign with 70. Sosa stalled near the finish line and wound up with 66—30 more home runs than he'd hit the previous season.

In *American Pastoral*, Philip Roth identified a homegrown varietal of hysteria he deemed the "American berserk," and the contemporary dialogue surrounding the home run seems to speak to that anxiety—America's gobbling ambition, its voraciousness, the muscly sense that to grind a ball into dust is a better and more exclamatory statement than a run scored piecemeal, through guile, sacrifice, and base hits.

It's always been there, of course, or at least since Babe Ruth's home run revolution. Yankees teammates Maris and Mickey Mantle followed in Ruth's footsteps in the 1960s, and in the '70s Orioles manager Earl Weaver preached the value of "pitching, defence, and the three-run home run."

In the anti-intellectual atmosphere of post-9/11 America, though, the swift and brutal rip through the strike zone seemed more appropriate than ever. Swinging for the fences became a primary characteristic of the game, a trend that continues today and which doesn't figure to go away. The homer has become too revered, taken on too big a profile, assumed too great an importance in the game as it's played now, to allow us to step wholly back. If the age of shock and awe deserved Barry Bonds, our even more dire-seeming age is perhaps best exemplified by Yankees slugger Aaron Judge, a human built on a different scale than you and I, with a swing that leaves no space for nuance.

This is all to say that sacrifice bunts don't attract contemporary viewers. They lack the inherent violence of the home run, the assertion of power, the unmistakable muscle. A base hit is accretive and team-oriented; it suggests faith in the hitters behind you. The home run is individual and ego-focused, one player's blood, bone, and sinew held aloft to deafening cheers.

In the face of that hegemony, any player who succeeds while bucking that trend becomes instantly notable. Enter Ichiro Suzuki. Ichiro arrived in America in the midst of what's now called the Steroid Era, his rookie campaign coinciding with Bonds's 73-homer year, as a fleet and wiry outfielder who never hit more than 15 in a season. Of his 3,089 Major League hits, fewer than 4 percent were home runs. He was content to let others hit dingers, as he believed he could be of more value to his team by consistently getting on base. It's a belief in a game played a different way, in a fading style; with Ichiro, one of its greatest proponents, no longer playing, a style that will perhaps soon disappear altogether.

His choice was apparently just that. Ichiro *could* hit home runs; he hit them every day in batting practice, ringing them off facades and video boards, sending them ricocheting off empty seats, inspiring the awe of teammates with balls that landed in unlikely places. No less an authority than Bonds himself declared that Ichiro would win any home run derby he entered, "easy, hands down."

But once the batting cage was wheeled away and the game's first pitch had been delivered, Ichiro was metronomic in his production: base hit after base hit, swinging for the gaps between fielders and not for the wall, steady and patient, the hits piling up, the faith in the hitters behind him dependable even when the hitters themselves were not. It was his game, and he played it that way for nineteen seasons, contrary to the prevailing fashion. While everybody else did their best to emulate the Babe, Ichiro was out there doing his best George Sisler.

At this point, arguing against the home run is pointless. The results are in and brawn has won—both in the ratings and on the field—and now, squarely within the launch angle era, the essential violence of the act hints that baseball's ostensible pastorality was misquoted, or ill understood, or more darkly still, a craven dishonesty.

A study in 2018 found that the balls put into use three years earlier, while not *juiced*, per se, were mysteriously more aerodynamic than they used to be, resulting in yet another spike in home runs: 6,105 were hit in 2017, more than in any previous season. That record, in turn, was pushed aside in 2019, when 6,776 homers were recorded. Also in 2019, when both Triple-A leagues switched from their own unique Chinese-manufactured balls to the very same Costa Rican-made balls used in Major League Baseball, home run totals across both leagues jumped 57 percent.

But it's not just what you hit, it's where you do the hitting. When Safeco Field opened in 1999, it had one of the most spacious outfields in baseball, with the centre-field fence sitting 409 feet from home plate, and the power alleys deeper than most parks, measuring 390 feet to left-centre field and 386 to right centre. The dimensions depressed the Mariners offensive numbers and thus drew complaints, and the walls were eventually moved in to make the park more hitter-friendly. In contrast, the original home of the Boston Red Sox at the Huntington Avenue Grounds measured 635 feet to centre in 1908. Clearly, it hosted a different game.

One has the sense that Ichiro could have played there, or in any of that age's vast and poorly maintained fields, and found just as much success as he did in the modern game. In fact, given his foot speed, he might even have been credited with more home runs; picture him placing a ball over a fielder's head to see it rattle around those pitted, pre-Turf Builder yards as he scampered all the way around the bases and home again. But arriving as he did during the most homer-happy time in the game's history, he defied that new orthodoxy, engaged in a thrillingly anachronistic style of play that made him, in part, the player he was: un-American, funky, an outsider, a player apart. A visitor from a distant era, inaccessible now, and never to return.

→→→⋘⋘

Understand, please, that I do not hate the home run.

I ramble around my house, often alone, often talking to myself, and usually, when in season, with a ballgame on—on a TV or a tablet or a laptop, whether the radio broadcast or the TV feed. I move from room to room and at times my attention is only loosely or partially on the action of the game. But then comes the telltale rise in the announcer's voice that presages a ball landing somewhere beyond the fence, and depending on who hit the ball, or which jersey they're wearing, I will celebrate. But I come from a long line of people who, when confronted with joy, tend to look it dead in the eye and say, "But what is it you *really* want?"

Understand, too, that I am not suggesting that the urge to gain competitive advantage via the use of salves, unguents, creams, pills, powders, or injected solutions is a new one. I'm aware that ballplayers have been dabbling in testosterone, amphetamines, and various snake oils since there was money to be made from winning ball games.

But when science caught up with desire, it began to change baseball in dramatic ways. José Canseco is the most glaring representation of that collision. He and his Oakland A's teammate, Mark McGwire, were named Rookie of the Year in 1986 and '87, respectively, and, for their combined slugging power were saddled with the goofily era-appropriate "Bash

Brothers" sobriquet. They bashed a lot of home runs, and the A's made a habit of appearing in the World Series.

Canseco, as it happened, was as brittle as he was bombastic, and the duo dissolved in 1992 when he was traded to the Rangers. McGwire kept hitting homers at a decent pace right up until he was traded to the Cardinals during the '97 season.

The following season, McGwire and the Cubs' Sammy Sosa went on their historic tear. By then, however, it was common knowledge that at least part of McGwire's success was due to his admitted use of the steroid androstenedione. Sosa, too, became the subject of suspicion, though it should be noted that, unlike McGwire, no one spied a smoking gun in his locker.

In 1998, androstenedione was not on Major League Baseball's list of banned substances (though it was banned by the International Olympic Committee), an important distinction, albeit a pretty fine one to make. So while not technically illegal at the time, it was still considered at best a little off, like a ringing double that smudges the foul line, and at worst an act of bad faith. Its usage was also increasingly commonplace. The use of supplements and performance enhancers was, in the estimation of 1996 National League MVP and admitted user Ken Caminiti, practised by half of all major leaguers.

The effects of androstenedione were stark. Big hitters like McGwire went from 30 or 40 homers a year to 60-plus, while fringe major leaguers with spotty or varied employment histories suddenly became 30-home-run guys, or even All-Stars. I grew up cheering for the Blue Jays, and I recall the happiness in knowing that Jesse Barfield's 40 homers led all hitters in 1986, or that the following season George Bell was named MVP when he hit 47. Fast forward just a decade and those numbers seem shockingly pedestrian.

Home runs are fine in isolation, or even in modest abundance. But in superabundance they tend to lose a bit of their appeal, to induce the roiling stomach I associate with the consumption of empty calories. The game's inherent balance, like my middle-age gut's precarious bacterial equilibrium, is thrown uncomfortably out of whack by too much of even the most delicious confection.

It's a bit simplistic, though, to suggest the Steroid Era is a stain on the game's history. It is, to be sure, a reminder that in a collision of faith and capitalism, capitalism almost inevitably triumphs. But labelling it an aberration feels uncomfortably close to laying all the blame at the feet of players, when the truth is that the history of baseball is characterized by efforts to streamline the flow of money toward those in control. Rest assured that during the 1990s home run boom, all concerned—players, owners, agents, networks, advertisers—were reaping the windfall of increased gate revenue and greater viewership. After the 1994 labour stoppage alienated a large number of paying fans, baseball succeeded in reentering the zeitgeist thanks to the record number of balls leaving big league yards all over America. Even though everybody seemed quite aware of the manner in which performance-enhancing substances were changing the game, nobody seemed terrifically interested in doing anything about it.

Not until Barry Bonds of the San Francisco Giants, a man who appeared to be driven in large measure by anger, surpassed McGwire and hit 73 home runs in 2001, at the age of thirty-seven. Arguably, things were threatening to verge on the utterly absurd, and Major League Baseball and the players' union eventually agreed to a drug-testing regime. Finally, it appeared that baseball had engaged in a process of rigorous self-examination, a holding to account, and the question of the legitimacy of players' accomplishments—and our collective faith therein—could be restored going forward.

It would, however, be premature to suggest that the era has been tied off tidily. Indeed, though the game footage of McGwire and Sosa has taken on the washed and grainy patina of deteriorating video tape, none of it has really gone away.

The Sosas and the McGwires and the Cansecos attracted a lot of attention, but most of the players caught up in the net of the Mitchell Report, baseball's official investigation into the use of performance-enhancing drugs, were not world-beaters or record-setters; they were middle-of-the pack guys looking to hold on, desperate to extend their careers in the face of injury or physical degradation. The dream of baseball stardom is, like all dreams, one that changes incrementally. First you dream of being Babe Ruth. Then you dream of making a roster. Then you dream of keeping a job.

But for those superstars and record holders—the would-be Hall of Famers—being implicated in the steroid conundrum has placed them (and us) in a holding pattern. As easy as it has become to wish away Bonds and Roger Clemens, who've acted their parts as villains, we're left to deal with their numerous accomplishments. Bonds hit 762 home runs while being named MVP a record seven times, and Clemens was awarded seven Cy Young Awards. Our desire to condemn and assign blame is complicated too by our implicit understanding that what occurred, and is still occurring, may not represent a moral failing so much as a talented ballplayer bowing to the cold exigencies of the baseball economy to which we all contribute.

It's generally our hope that some exceptional expression of character accompanies our ballplayers' GIF-able highlights. But in most cases we must remain content when they perform their duty to its strict letter—when they show up, don the uniform, move the runners over, throw strikes, hit the cut-off man. And maybe that's enough. Maybe we don't want to know how the sausage is made. But it's worth remembering, even as we continue to suffer the disappointing news of failed drug tests like that of Robinson Canó in late 2020, that the players alone did not write the tune to which they danced.

In this, as in so many other things, it occurs to me how like our lives baseball can be—how complicated, how ambiguous, how unsure it can make us of our own judgment. And that happiness, when found, is frequently multilayered and slippery, and should all too often be interrogated.

Baseball reflects our desires, a frequently sorrowful and occasionally joyful exercise that feels endless in the moment but short and ephemeral in hindsight. It possesses visual suggestions of timelessness—rolling fields, pennants snapping in the breeze, pinstripes, stirrups, leather belts—but is in fact in a constant process of change. The modern power game did not arise spontaneously, but expresses a contemporary desire for bombast and dominance.

It happens sometimes that we move toward something to which we are attracted, believing that more of it will make us happier, or fuller, or better. And in rare moments, in that pursuit, we catch sight of our own reflection, not believing that the unflattering sight is us, though it most certainly is.

I can't wrap my head around what it must have been like to show up to work every day for members of the 2003 Detroit Tigers. What must it have taken, as the losses mounted—up to and including the 119th, the most defeats ever amassed by an American League team, and just one win better than the 1962 Mets, losers of the most games in major league history—to rouse oneself for the excruciating daily repetition of a very public abasement?

Alan Trammell was one of the best shortstops of his generation and, along with Lou Whitaker, half of one of the sweetest and surest double-play combinations in history, as well as a vital member of the 1984 champion Tigers team. What was it like for Tram to oversee the disastrous 2003 season from his manager's post in the dugout?

What must it have felt like to suffer the hundredth loss of the season, only to look at the calendar and realize it was not yet even September?

Dmitri Young was the best hitter the Tigers had that year, an All-Star for what that's worth, who toiled valiantly to put up decent numbers amid all the frustration, clubhouse shenanigans, and interpersonal acrimony. How aware was Young of the glacial nature of time from August 30 until the final day of that campaign? A month spent as a hundred-game loser. Waking up with that. Playing through that. Going to bed with that in his head.

Such a brutal gauntlet would daunt the staunchest among us, but it's an excellent, if extreme, example of how baseball-time works. Because baseball time, inescapably, moves so slowly that it seems to tinker with the basic mechanics of the universe. Stubbornly, as everything else accelerates until it begins to blur into abstraction, this stupid game—despite every effort to speed it up—remains befuddlingly slow. Slowness is baked right into the marrow and blood of it all. Frantic, ecstatic bursts of energy do stud the proceedings, but these are the exception to the rule. That's why they're so damn exciting. Scarcity breeds demand.

My kids are just beginning to grasp all this. Pity them, for they have been born into this. I have undermined their defences since each arrived in this world, and they have only known a home in which baseball is revered, its apparent flaws held aloft as proof of its sublime design.

➤➤➤◄◄◄

The boys and I happened by a field near here—a beautiful diamond, with all the bells and whistles, partially paid for by the Toronto Blue Jays' charitable foundation—as players were gathering ahead of a game. We had time to kill, so we took in the pregame protocols and routines, liturgical in their rigidity. Tarps were removed, pins were placed at home and at first and third. String was extended between these, and used as guides for the baselines, which were drawn in powdered chalk. The string and pins were removed, and stowed in a utility shed down along the first-base side of the park. Young men in uniforms began to saunter onto the field, filling the warm, thick air with the sound of balls landing in gloves. A pair of coaches occupied the line halfway between first base and the foul pole, one with a bat, the other a glove and a bucket of balls. Three young men stood approximately in centre. The coach with the bat tossed himself a ball and swung choppily, sending it arcing into the gathering dusk. One young man took four smooth steps, allowed the ball to settle cleanly into his glove, then transferred the ball to his throwing hand, coiled, and unwound a throw to the second coach, who fielded it and dumped it back into his bucket. Repeat, repeat, repeat. The other team's players were sprinting half-heartedly from the left field line to a spot near second base. In the bullpen, a pitcher warmed up. Elsewhere, young men—they were maybe fourteen years old, fifteen, these players—stood around and joked and postured and swore. There was spitting. The aluminum bleachers filled. Parents came and erected their own folding chairs, chatted with one another, checked their phones for the practice schedule, the next game, planning their weeknights of quick dinners and drives and hours spent just this way, in these same folding chairs.

"Are they starting soon?" asked Theo, hoping we'd stay to watch. I asked a man nearby. He checked his watch. "Forty-five minutes," he said. We sat and talked about the Blue Jays while the sunlight aged and the shadows lengthened and softened until finally the lamps atop their stanchions provided the majority of the illumination.

Summer, we call this. Nothing of consequence happened for long stretches, giving us time to roll in our mouths the game's beautiful language—Baltimore chop, Texas Leaguer, can of corn, dying quail, fungo, eephus—and pass between us a bag of sunflower seeds.

The young men pitched and swung and caught and threw. The mosquitoes set in. Traffic whooshed by. At some point, almost without our knowing it, an umpire appeared and a proper game congealed. The players aligned into formation and a recognizable order was established. We clapped, leaned forward, tried to guess what would happen next.

Innings passed (two? five?) and I told the boys we had to leave. None of us knew the score. None of us could name the teams. We'd simply stumbled onto a game, taken some of it in, and moved on. We'd do the same again soon, there or at some other park. The chance constitutes much of the appeal. That, and the way time, in deference to the heat and the nature of the game, goes sticky, stretches, comes to resemble something other than itself.

After loss number 100 but before number 119, Christie and I found ourselves at Comerica Park, taking in a game between the Tigers and Cleveland. What can I say? We are drawn to historic, flamboyant, catastrophic displays of failure. More to the point, she and I, having early in our relationship attended one last, glorious game at the beautiful wreck that was Tiger Stadium, wished to see this new park they'd built to replace it, and bought tickets high in the upper deck on the third-base side. At the outset of our road trip, the American border patrol agent, having inquired as to the purpose of our crossing, reacted with incredulity. His exact words, I believe, were, "You're going to see the Tigers?"

We ate dinner somewhere near the Fox Theater and then strolled over to the stadium, snapped photos of the giant tiger statues flanking the front gate. In one, Christie is wearing a navy blue Tigers batting practice jersey that had somehow come into her possession, the old English D in orange on the chest, her hair in pigtails, glasses sliding down her nose, while one of the stone tigers lifts its clawed foot over her head and snarls.

We walked lazily around the concourse, saw the carousel and the Ferris wheel, bought beers and hot dogs. We mounted the ramps to the upper deck and took our seats, where we ate popcorn and put our feet up on the empty seatbacks in front of us. We clapped and hollered as a soft dusk fell over the empty shell of downtown Detroit. The game wrapped up—8–6 Tigers, just their 35th win of the year, with Young hitting a solo homer—and then we found the car and retreated to our motel room. The next morning we drove home. Sometime thereafter the Tigers lost their 119th game. Blessedly, the end came on a cool, cloudy Sunday afternoon, in front of an announced crowd of 18,959 home fans who were on hand, it feels it safe to assume, both to say goodbye to a miserable season and to see if the home side would set a modern record for futility.

It could have been worse, if you can believe it. Animated by desperation, or maybe just luck, the Tigers won their last two games and five of their last six. The season ended. Everyone moved on.

If you're Dmitri Young and it's the tail end of September and you're forty-nine games behind the Twins with two to play, what do you do with that? One more loss and that's it, you're officially the losingest losers to ever take the field. What the hell does a person do with that? You continue to show up is what you do. You show up and you win one lousy fucking game and you go home and sleep and then you show up again the next day, because there are winners and there are losers and, among all this world's sad and unenviable fates, at least you're in the goddamn game.

# PEDRO GUERRERO

I've been thinking about Pedro Guerrero lately. While doing some personal archaeology in a neglected drawer, I unearthed an old button bearing his smiling face on the front, and his 1984 batting average—.303—on the reverse. It was produced as part of a series of similar buttons by the Fun Foods company, and I got it in a thrift store in Port Angeles, Washington, while waiting for a ferry in August 2001.

I know that I used to wear it on a corduroy coat that was a couple sizes too big for me, reinforcing the impression that I was unfinished, or still had room to grow. This was a lot of years ago, though the above might still be true.

⟶⟩⟨⟨⟵

Baseball brainiac Bill James once called Guerrero "The best hitter God had made in a long time." On NBC *Game of the Week* broadcasts, or while calling Dodger games for the SoCal radio market, Vin Scully called him "Pete."

More than most players, examining Guerrero's life feels like voyeurism. When he was good, he was, as James suggested, astonishingly good. He was big and strong, and had a quick right-handed bat, throwing the head violently through the zone. When he made contact sometimes it seemed like he might knock a Soyuz-T out of orbit.

But his bad times were difficult to watch, and they lacked the privacy we all hope will shelter our worst moments. This was a result, at least in part, of his place of employment. He was plucked out of poverty in San Pedro de Macoris by Cleveland, traded to the Dodgers, and dropped into the swirling and too-bright opulence of 1980s Los Angeles, where he and everyone around him were rewarded for excess and impulsivity. That same momentum carried him into the '90s, but as his celebrity and skillset faded, he seemed unable to locate the brake. He went from sharing the MVP honours in the 1981 World Series and being a five-time All-Star—feats his employers enjoyed enough to make him the highest-paid Dodger of all time when he signed a five year, seven million dollar contract in 1984—to vaulting a table to throw punches at Todd Worrell, taking the fall for fronting money to buy fifteen kilos of cocaine from an undercover agent in Miami, and, possibly, doing drugs with O. J.'s girlfriend.

---

A part of me now worries that the latter half of that list is what I was referencing by wearing that pin on my secondhand XL corduroy coat. In those days I traded in irony, the crueller the better. I was in my twenties and it was the twentieth century's last gasp, and that's what a lot of us did. We celebrated things that were plainly bad as supremely good. In that last pre-9/11 summer, when the world was a bit more slapdash and improvised than it was to become, cynicism was a currency still rare enough to be trading high. It was still, and I beg you to forgive me the use of this word, edgy.

When Guerrero went to trial for that drug deal, his lawyer argued that his client was intellectually incapable of recognizing the consequences of his actions. That his defense worked, and Guerrero walked free, does not rob the tactic of its cruelty, nor restore Guerrero's dignity in the face of the justice system's impersonal workings.

I'm trying to remember how I greeted that news. Did I find it funny? Was Pedro Guerrero a joke to me?

---

It's true that Guerrero had trouble hiding his emotions. He threatened Nolan Ryan once, and the Express responded by cracking his batting helmet with a fastball. But it's also true that Guerrero had a lot to be upset about. With all the promise he'd shown, he lost a sizeable portion of his career to injury. That would frustrate and disappoint most of us, and Pedro did not hide his disappointment in himself, in the world. It manifested in weight gain, poor effort, conspicuous consumption, emotional outbursts. He threw a bat at David Cone. He lashed out at umpires, reporters, teammates. He could be error-prone and guilty of lapses. His hitting would fail at crucial moments, he would throw behind a runner. Inevitably, the fans would get on him and the press would have questions. "Everybody hates the Dodgers," he answered.

And then in 1988, just months before the Dodgers won their second World Series of the decade, Los Angeles traded Guerrero to the Cardinals. He responded first by suggesting the Dodgers owed him more than the half-share of the World Series bonus they sent him, and then by having a hell of a year in 1989, hitting .311, knocking in 117 runs, racking up 42 doubles, and landing in that summer's All-Star Game.

Like a lot of us, I spent my twenties trying to distance myself from the child I'd only recently been. Things that had once given me solace came to look a lot like simple juvenile distractions. And even the things I could not bear to abandon—baseball, mostly—I found new ways to accommodate. Instead of innocence and hope, I viewed them with cynicism and sarcasm.

I couldn't bear to face the game sincerely. I'd loved it too much, and was too bound up in it. It was too involved in how I'd presented myself to the world. To nakedly accept something as earnest and nostalgia-laden as baseball would be to put myself on display with no embellishment, no armour, and I was not prepared to do that. Instead I revelled in others' mistakes and I spoke sarcastically about the thing I loved and I embraced a player like Guerrero as a symbol of absurdity and vice. I wore that pin without ever pausing to consider the man's humanity.

At some point I took the pin off and I buried it in a drawer, where it sat in darkness for over a decade, until I dug it out. The corduroy coat to which it was affixed is long gone.

--->>><<<---

By 1993 Guerrero's baseball peak was well and truly behind him. He could not secure a spot in the majors, or even in the affiliated minors, so he signed with the Sioux Falls Canaries of the independent Northern League, and then the Charros de Jalisco of the Mexican League. Far from the dazzle of Hollywood, he found himself in baseball's most distant provinces. He spun his wheels for a couple years before finally conceding the obvious and retiring in 1995.

He'd been a rare talent, but talent only gets you so far. Injuries took years off Guerrero's career, and the Dodgers held him in the minors too long, because every position he might have played was already occupied. Then, once he arrived in the bigs, Pedro Guerrero was drunk much of the time. "I used to come to the park with a hangover every day," he's said. And it's hard not to look at that, and at the impetuousness he sometimes displayed, and label the entirety of his career a missed opportunity.

Things changed in retirement. Guerrero dried out, found God, began mentoring children, and eventually achieved success as a manager in the Mexican Northern League. In recent photos, Guerrero is almost always smiling.

--->>><<<---

In 2015, while back home in the Dominican Republic, he suffered a stroke, and then, in 2017, he had a second one in New York, after which doctors declared him brain-dead.

I've spent some time in a hospital recently, by my mother's bedside while she recovered from cancer surgery. This is the other reason I have been thinking of Pedro Guerrero. The wires and tubes, the hum of machines, the soft electronic tone denoting an abnormal reading, the unflappable ICU nurse at the ready, moving calmly to comfort, to assess. In the low artificial light of three in the morning and amid the fog of my mother's narcotic confusion, I thought back to another hospital, and to the time spent between our twin boys' beds when they—tiny, premature, and precarious—fought their way through the first month of their lives. I thought of the strange way time moves in those places, waiting to hear from doctors, when boredom mingles with fear, and the worst thing any of us can think about is so proximate.

Guerrero's wife, Roxanna, held out hope. A further exam revealed that he was not, in fact, brain dead, but in a deep coma. Still, doctors were pessimistic and recommended taking him off life support. Roxanna refused. Two days later he awoke, and shortly after that he walked out of the hospital.

When are we our real selves? Do the changes we make later in life reflect something about the people we've been all along, or at least suggest that we'd always had it in us to be that newer version? And what accounts for that change? Do external factors knock us into some new personhood, or are we the people we are regardless of our experiences?

What I'm asking is: can a photo reproduced on a button in 1984 signify two people at once?

Here's an experiment: write down all the events of Guerrero's life—the accomplishments, the lows, the stories written, the words exchanged—on a set of cards, without his name on any of them. Lay them out in any order and look them over. Does your eye alight on the highs and then on the hard times, and do you then measure the gulf between them? Do you shake your head and say, "This person had *everything*." Or do you maybe muse something along the lines of, "This person had everything stacked against him." Because whichever of those two reactions his story inspires, if Pedro Guerrero could hear you, I'm willing to bet he'd agree.

# ICHIRO SUZUKI,
## THE STAR OF BASEBALL

I've had an email account since about 1992—a span of nearly thirty uninterrupted years. The first was a National Capital FreeNet account, non-personalized, which was, if I'm remembering correctly, two alphabetical characters, followed by several digits. It was more license plate than personal identifier. Access was via dial-up modem, of course.

I've been alive more years with the internet than without it. I've written for the internet, and been employed populating small corners of it. I've used it to conduct vast amounts of research. I watch baseball on it, and make phone calls through it. And yet, for reasons I can't quite articulate, when thinking about how things work, or the way things are, I default to a pre-connected world—like favouring the road atlas we keep rolled up next to the driver's seat over GPS or Google Maps. The internet still feels new to me. It still feels nascent.

So there's a bit of a sense of disconnect when I stumble across something that reminds me just how long the internet has been a part of my life. Such was the case when, while hunting down some scrap of Ichiro-related minutiae, I stumbled across a fansite called ICHIRO SUZUKI, THE STAR OF BASEBALL. It's a little bit of the early aughts preserved in amber.

I don't have to tell you that time on the internet is not measured as it is IRL. I literally have, and continue to wear, items of clothing older than ICHIRO SUZUKI, THE STAR OF BASEBALL. But internet-time is accelerated to such an absurd degree that a website from a decade and a half ago—just about the time Christie and I were married—represents an opportunity to peek through the geological ages. It's digital archaeology.

The site features characteristic side-frame menus, rudimentary graphics, a wallpapered background, scrolling text, and a clunky Tripod-hosted URL. These basic things, miraculously, suggest to me a simpler time, or at least a less sophisticated internet, slower, boxier, and a great deal less integrated into our daily lives.

When ICHIRO SUZUKI, THE STAR OF BASEBALL was last regularly updated, not only was Ichiro a new sporting phenomenon in America, but the world was a different place. It was a time when low-rise jeans flourished, presumably because the iPhone had not yet been invented and so pocket space was not quite as necessary.

And the internet was different too, in great and largely inarticulable ways, from the one we use today. Digital communication is now so ubiquitous, and so fast, that it feels synaptic, embedded somewhere between thought and action, or desire and delivery. Then, it was the domain of the tech-savvy. It was frontier-like in its possibilities, and in its mannerisms cheerier and more innocent. We used it to talk about the things we liked. We berated less and enthused more.

In November of 2000, right around the time Ichiro signed his contract with the Mariners, someone called Wincey decided their admiration of Ichiro was strong enough to deserve regular updates in a public space. It's not such a strange thing to do now, and it wasn't so unusual then, either. We were lurching into this new world, and there was a limitless space to populate with our enthusiasms. A baseball player was a worthy subject for such a project. Given my diversions, I might have done the same thing. You might have too. This was before Twitter and its parody accounts, after all.

Sometime around the end of June 2003, though, Wincey decided to move on, as eventually we all must. They lost interest, or circumstances changed in such a way that prevented them from devoting attention to curating their little corner of the internet, providing the faceless masses with updates on Ichiro's ongoing MLB success. Then as now, personal web spaces, in their glorious and unruly abundance, bequeathed on their keepers an anonymity at once liberating and defeating.

That an inactive fansite should survive such a span of time—four presidential administrations, a pair of decades-long wars in the Middle East, the death of landlines, six *Star Wars* films—is not unremarkable. The internet is vast, and great swaths of it have succumbed to link rot, domain scrapers, and the churn of ISPs, but most of it remains, hidden only by the great volume of new content. Your Blogger site is still kicking around somewhere, as is your Myspace page. These digital presences accumulate as a matter of course, and as we abandon them they spread out behind us like a wake.

The online spaces that manage to survive time's onslaught represent a strange and poignant hybridity of permanence and ephemerality, the commingling of disposability and stubbornness. Like plastic, abandoned websites are here with us forever, even if they're no longer any good to us. They are for the most part quiet, but we encounter their intermittent pulsing from time to time, our attention drawn to them as to a smoke alarm with a low battery. They don't function properly anymore, but we place them under glass, as specimens, testimony of a prior age.

At Wincey's last update, the Mariners' next scheduled game was against the Anaheim Angels, Freddy Garcia matching up against Aaron Sele. The Mariners would win that game, 6–4, with both starters factoring in the decision. Ichiro would go 2-for-4, raising his average to .358, and score a run.

As Pompeii was trapped in the ash and pumice of Vesuvius, so does Wincey's website freeze Ichiro in place, a day in the life remarkable for how representative it was and would continue to be. A single and a double in four at-bats. Two hits out of 3,089 he'd earn in MLB, or, if you prefer the wider scope of his career, out of 4,367. A Tuesday night game against a division rival before 39,000 fans at what was then called Edison Field in Anaheim. It was cloudy. The temperature at first pitch was 69°F. Just another game, number 75 of 162 for the Mariners, but also a testament to Ichiro's long brilliance when you consider that he had very similar results in games ten, twelve, fifteen years after Wincey last updated the site.

What's further remarkable about Wincey's page is the testimony it provides regarding Ichiro's peculiar stardom. Were there similar pages devoted to Manny Ramirez? To Roger Clemens? The collision of east and west in the person of Ichiro, and the topography of his career, encouraged the cross-pollination of communities. There's a creativity and flamboyance to Japanese baseball fandom, one suggested by THE STAR OF BASEBALL, that isn't endemic to American rooting. Attending a baseball game in North America got incrementally more interesting after Ichiro's debut, and efforts like Wincey's digital praise of number 51 contributed to that.

So the value of the page isn't solely resident in the information it preserves. That's all available elsewhere. Rather, the site, and untold numbers of others like it—one-time testaments to fandom—now function as commentary on insubstantiality in the age of digital memory, of time and its passage. Here is something I once loved, it says, and this was the manner in which that love was once expressed, mawkish and amateur though it might appear now. Here is how it looked and felt to be enmeshed in the warp and woof of this thing.

But all ages pass; everything is surpassed. The world innovates and evolves, and today's sophistication is tomorrow's punchline. That's the whisper beneath the page name's all-caps shout. One day all of this will look innocent too. Ichiro aged and retired, as unthinkable as that once was, and his deeds have passed into history. Now, all accounts of his import and effect are secondhand at best, awkward testimonials gesturing at what it all meant, but layered beneath time and the passing of codes, beliefs, ways of doing. As immovable and constant as Ichiro has so long been, he is in the process of becoming what was. Count on it.

## SPOKE, PECK, AND THE GREATEST BASEBALL GAME EVER PLAYED IN PETERBOROUGH

If there's anything that beats live baseball, it's free live baseball. Accordingly, on certain summer evenings when fortune or luck provides us with a break between kids' sports practices and games, meetings, and other sundry commitments, we make our way across town to East City.

Peterborough, Ontario sits on the Otonabee River, which runs from the town of Lakefield in the north, down to Rice Lake, which in turn flows into the Trent River, which empties into Lake Ontario. The city of Peterborough is cleaved in two by the Otonabee, and the land to the east of the river was once the separate town of Ashburnham, until it was swallowed up by Peterborough in the early twentieth century. In the years that followed the former town came to be referred to locally as East City. It's there, at the foot of the marvellously arched Hunter Street Bridge, that we go to watch free ball.

There's a Circle K convenience store across the street, so I parallel park the minivan and we go in to buy bags of flavoured sunflower seeds and enormous eighty-seven cent insulated cups—tubs, really—of soda. Dr. Pepper for me, and ungodly combinations of all flavours on offer for the kids. Then we cross Burnham Street to find some seats.

The East City Bowl is a ball diamond cut into the hill at the base of the bridge, with permanent bleacher seating built against the sharp incline behind home and down toward first. The arrangement makes this small community park feel somehow both larger and more intimate than most other parks its size. Home plate aligns with the intersection of Hunter and Burnham Streets. The diamond's all-dirt infield is ringed by a well-tended grass outfield. A chain-link fence describes a clean arc from foul pole to foul pole, and is decorated with the names and numbers of people who've played here, jerseys painted on plywood. Over the fence in left lies the Lions Club. Beyond centre rises the tall backstop of a second, larger diamond, just to the southwest. Past that a mature deciduous curtain suggests the river's edge. Crane your neck from a bleacher seat down the first base line and take in the Quaker Oats factory on the other side of the bridge, imposing brickishly over the town, its white water tower a beacon and its warm, sweet oatmeal scent a source of comfort to people who call this place home.

We settle into the spots we've chosen and set our eyes on a game, often already in progress. Sometimes it's boys playing baseball, sometimes it's girls playing fastpitch softball. It doesn't matter to us. We crack seeds, slurp from our large, slushy drinks, and take it in. The sun sinks into pastel softness over downtown Peterborough, moths and June bugs flutter around the floodlights, and the crowd—on the bleachers, or in chairs they've brought with them and placed in the grass down the left-field line—clap, chat with neighbours, and sip from Tim's cups. It's a Monday or a Wednesday or a Thursday evening in June or July or August, and there are far worse places to be.

Eventually I'll say it. I won't be able to stop myself, even though I know the kids know it, and Christie knows it. They've all heard it before.

"You know," I say dutifully, "Tris Speaker played a game here."

Tristram Edgar Speaker was born in Hubbard, Texas, on April 4, 1888, the first year of operation for the Texas League, where the outfielder would begin his professional career eighteen years later. In 1907 he was sold to Boston of the still-new American League—a team that wouldn't be known as the Red Sox until the following season, when a young Speaker hit a lowly .224. Spoke, as he was known, became the team's everyday centre fielder in 1909, and his hitting improved significantly. He would eventually become one of the best hitters in the game, achieving a lifetime mark of .345, still the sixth-best career average of all time. His defense was extraordinary; as a centre fielder he was considered without peer, routinely playing so shallow that he could converse with the middle infielders, and then when a ball was struck turning to gallop to the spot where he would collect the ball at a dead run. He once chased down a Joe Jackson fly ball and crashed into the fence, knocking himself out. The ball remained in his glove.

Spoke won two World Series titles with the Red Sox, in 1912 and 1915. He was instrumental to that second championship, though his average slipped to .322, 16 points under his 1914 showing. Boston team owner Joseph Lannin demanded Speaker take a pay cut as a result. Speaker refused, so on April 8, 1916, he was traded to Cleveland.

The best hitter of the day was Ty Cobb, who had won nine batting titles in a row coming into the 1916 season. Speaker hit .386 that year with Cleveland and wrestled the crown from Cobb, a nice bit of thanks-for-the-memories directed Boston's way. In 1919 Speaker became Cleveland's manager while continuing to patrol the outfield at spacious Dunn Field. The following season he led the team to a World Series victory, batting .388 with a league-best 50 doubles. Cobb wound up with a .334 average, a down year for him, on a seventh-place Tigers squad. Their competitive impulses notwithstanding, Speaker and Cobb were friends, insofar as Cobb, a notoriously difficult personality, could be said to have any.

There's a photo of Spoke in a Cleveland uniform, relaxed, foot resting on the running board of a parked sedan. Facebook populated my feed with it one day several years ago, back when I was still on Facebook. It had been posted without accompanying information by our local museum and archive with a handful of other photos connected only by their deteriorating condition. It was shortly before Halloween, and the idea was that the state of degradation made these commonplace photos—of a ballplayer, children, buildings—in some way sinister.

The ballplayer didn't look creepy in the least. He looked proud. He looked severe. He looked like someone I should be able to name, but couldn't. What I could identify was the setting: it looked an awful lot like George Street in downtown Peterborough, about two miles from my house.

I shared the photo, captioning it "WHO IS THIS?" My friend and fiction editor Bryan Ibeas—primarily a basketball man—replied in short order: "Isn't that Tris Speaker?"

I did a quick photo search and confirmed that it was Speaker, then reached out to the archives, but they didn't have any more information. The photo had come to them unlabelled in a batch from a local photography studio.

The photo was dated October 1923. The *Peterborough Examiner* has published continuously since 1847, and the vast majority of its issues are still archived at the Peterborough Public Library. If I wanted to know what a Hall of Fame centre fielder was doing in uniform on George Street in 1923, I was going to have to dig into the microfiche collection.

Just days after Cleveland's 1923 season had ended with a 9–6 win over the White Sox, Speaker hit the road with a barnstorming squad, an amalgam of players he generously titled Speaker's American League All-Stars, and while the group included a pair of genuine stars—namely, Speaker and Cobb—the roster was filled out with lesser-known big leaguers, such as George Burns of Boston, Jim Edwards of Cleveland, and catcher Les Nunamaker who'd retired the previous season after four years each with the Red Sox, Yankees, and Cleveland, and one with the St. Louis Browns. The rest of the team was populated with minor leaguers, the most noteworthy of whom was the Hamilton-born Babe Dye, who excelled at baseball, football, and hockey, helping the Toronto

St. Patricks win the 1922 Stanley Cup. He was inducted into the Hockey Hall of Fame in 1970.

The *Examiner* first mentioned this travelling road show on Thursday, October 11, 1923, heralding a game to be held the following Saturday afternoon between Speaker's team and Conny Burns's Toronto Wellingtons. The All-Stars, said the uncredited piece, would be "motored in from Toronto," and would feature "well known players, while the Wellingtons will have a classy squad of clever performers."

An ad in Friday's *Examiner* touted the contest as "the Greatest Baseball Game Ever Played in Peterborough," pitting "American Stars vs. Wellington Semi-Pro. Team of Toronto," to be played at Riverside Park, "Peterboro." The front page featured a joint headline: "YANKEES WIN SECOND 4–2 / SPEAKER'S "ALL STARS" HERE TO-MORROW."

On the left side of the front page was the first of several pages of World Series coverage, including a photo of the Giants' Frankie Frisch getting caught stealing second, and another of Babe Ruth, mid-swing, looking classically Ruthian. It was the third straight year that the Yankees and Giants faced off for all the marbles, with John McGraw's Giants taking the 1921 and '22 crowns. In 1923, however, at precisely the moment the *Examiner*'s readers were gearing up for Speaker's visit, the balance was tipping. The Yankees, playing their first year at Yankee Stadium, were on the verge of beating their crosstown rivals in six games, the first of the mighty franchise's titles. The Age of Ruth was underway.

The copy in the *Examiner*'s right-hand front page column that day read, "This is an unique chance to see some of the Nabobs of baseball in action, including Speaker, Roger Peckinpaugh, Babe Dye, Jim Edward[s], Andy Anderson, and others."

To see so much ink devoted to baseball coverage comes as no surprise when you consider the sport's esteem in 1923 in both the United States and Canada. Baseball was *the* summer game in small towns on either side of the border. The earliest documented game of baseball took place in Beachville, Ontario, in 1838—eighty-five years before Tris Speaker brought his All-Stars north. The first organized game in Peterborough was staged on the shores of Little Lake on September 9, 1876, between a team from Cavanville and the Peterborough Pine Grove Baseball Club. Other nineteenth-century teams in the area included the Ashburnham Astonishers, the Peterborough Silver Star Baseball Team, and the Excelsiors. The Electric City was a town full of skilled ballplayers and smart, passionate cranks.

That was true of a lot of places, of course, and it does little to explain the All-Stars' Canadian itinerary: just two games, one in east-end Toronto and then, a few days later, Peterborough. Though something of a regional hub, the site of a decent ballyard, and a gateway to the outdoor paradise of the Kawartha Lakes, it seems unlikely that Speaker would choose this town of barely twenty-thousand mosquito-bitten souls, in what the Ojibwe named "the place at the end of the rapids," and Catharine Parr Traill called "the bush."

But Speaker was an outdoorsman, which was almost certainly the draw. The Texan was an excellent marksman who possessed an expert duck call, and was said to have taught Will Rogers how to use a lasso. He hunted everything, fished for anything, and loved to cook what he killed.

Shortly after he arrived in Cleveland following his trade from Boston, Speaker met Morris Ackerman, a columnist for the *Cleveland News*. The pair soon began hunting and fishing together, and it was common for Speaker to spend portions of his offseason on trips with friends and teammates in the woods or on rivers and lakes all over North America, from Texas to California to Wyoming to Ontario.

On at least two occasions, Speaker and Nunamaker, the catcher, ventured to Rainy Lake in the northern Kawarthas and, according to Timothy M. Gay's biography *Tris Speaker:*

*The Rough-and-Tumble Life of a Baseball Legend*, the centre fielder had a cabin on Idylwyld Island in Price Lake, Ontario. In 1921, Gay reports, "the local Hiawatha Indian tribe in the area… honored Speaker and his hunting and fishing buddy… Les Nunamaker, with a special dinner."

I can't find a Price Lake with an Idylwyld Island anywhere in Ontario. It's very possible that it exists—there are a quarter of a million lakes in this province. But if it exists (or existed), it's pulled off a very impressive disappearing act in the era of Google Maps; it might rather be that over time the names have been confused or jumbled.

Speaker's pal Ackerman refers to *Rice* Lake in a column dated shortly after Cleveland's 1920 Series win, and claims that Speaker along with Nunamaker, "Clay Folger, chief of detectives in charge of police protection at the Cleveland ball yard," and a fourth man spent ten days at Rice Lake in October of that year. "Their camp was pitched at Idlewild, an island in the middle of the lake," writes Ackerman.

A footnote to Speaker's—and Cobb's—1923 itinerary also proves useful. Thursday's *Examiner* reported the results of the exhibition match in Toronto, at "Scarboro Beach grounds," a 10–6 victory for the All-Stars. In describing the pregame ceremonies, it noted: "Just before the game started, Captain Thompson presented hunting and fishing licences to Speaker, Nunamaker, Cobb, Peckinpaugh and Edwards. These players are in Canada on a hunting trip, Speaker's party being headed for Rice Lake, near Peterborough."

Rice Lake, so named for the wild grain the Mississauga have long harvested there, is still an outdoor enthusiast's delight, lined with cottages and summer homes, humming with powerboats and popular for fishing. Situated on the lake's northern shore, very near where the Otonabee empties, then as now: the Hiawatha First Nation.

It's easy to imagine a simple typographical error or misheard dictation turning "Rice" into "Price" in a daily paper or some other account. Rice Lake, it seems safe to assert, was Speaker's northern base of recreational operations.

→→⊁⊰←←

Henry Calcutt was a brewer. He'd learned the trade from his father, James Calcutt of Queen's County, Ireland. Henry moved from Cobourg, Ontario, to Peterborough in 1855, married, and established his own brewing business in a building he leased. In time he built his own brewery in Ashburnham. He began a steamboat excursion company, ferrying tourists up and down the Otonabee to Rice Lake. Around 1875 he added to his budding empire, building a resort on Rice Lake to serve as the terminus to his steamships' excursions. He named it Idyll Wild.

Calcutt was also a community builder who, according to the Peterborough and District Sports Hall of Fame, believed in "the intrinsic value of sports in building character." He was president of the local lacrosse club, the local snowshoe club, and in 1885 he was president of the Peterborough Baseball Club. Adjacent to his brewery he built an indoor skating and curling rink for public use, in 1870. He later tore that down and in its place built the baseball diamond that Speaker would visit, the one that's still there now, where we crack seeds with our teeth and suck soda through straws the diameter of drainage culverts. The Lions Club building, out there beyond the left field foul pole, occupies the very spot his brewery once did.

Calcutt died in 1913, and his resort closed sometime in the early part of that century, so it's unlikely that he ever knew Speaker. But if I'm wrong about Rice Lake being the longtime seat of Speaker's Canadian adventures, there are still a whole lot of coincidences lined up, like zeroes in a perfect game.

And since I'm connecting dots, let's talk about Roger Peckinpaugh. Peck, as he was known, was a shortstop with the best throwing arm of his generation. Legendary *Washington*

*Post* baseball columnist Shirley Povich wrote, "The spectacle of Peckinpaugh, slinging himself after ground balls, throwing from out of position and nailing his man by half a step was an American League commonplace."

Born in Wooster, Ohio, Peck was still a child when his family moved to Cleveland. In high school he excelled in football, basketball, and baseball. At some point the boy caught the attention of Nap Lajoie, who lived nearby. So integral to the identity of Cleveland's AL club was Lajoie that the team, once called the Bronchos, was renamed Naps in his honour. When Nap spoke, ownership listened. The team signed Peckinpaugh in 1910 and sent him to New Haven in the Connecticut League. He spent the following year with the Pacific Coast League's Portland Beavers, and in 1912 the young shortstop was given his shot with the parent team.

His initial struggles convinced the Naps to hand the shortstop job to Ray Chapman, and in 1913 Peck was traded to the Yankees. New York had yet to blossom into the glorious winning franchise they would be for the majority of the century; the year Peck joined them they rang up 94 losses. Toward the end of 1914, another lousy season, manager Frank Chance stepped away from his duties and the reigns were handed to Peck on an interim basis. His level head seemed well suited to the role. "The calmest man in baseball," he was called and also, at twenty-three, the youngest ever to manage a big league team. The Yanks went ten and ten under his watch.

The Yankees slowly improved, aided in no small measure by the arrival of George Herman Ruth in 1920. In the 1921 World Series, a best-of-nine contest—the first of those three consecutive championships matching the Yankees and McGraw's Giants—Peck hit poorly and in the deciding game made a crucial error, allowing the National Leaguers to eke out the win, 1–0.

Ruth later complained that manager Miller Huggins's decisions were to blame, and that the team ought to consider replacing him with Peckinpaugh. The result was that owner Jacob Ruppert shipped Peck to the Red Sox, who then turned around a few weeks later and included the shortstop in a three-way deal with Philadelphia and Washington. Peck became a Senator.

With Washington, Peckinpaugh formed a solid double-play combination with second baseman Bucky Harris. In 1924 Harris was appointed player-manager, and the Senators claimed the AL pennant in '24 and '25. The Sens bested the Giants in seven games in the first of Washington's consecutive Series appearances, with Peck hitting .417 and providing the winning hit in Game Two. He was slowed in later games by injury, but still provided sparkling defense.

The 1925 Series was a different story. Peck had a hell of a season and was named the AL MVP for his all-around play, but in October he fell apart against the Pirates. The usually solid shortstop committed eight errors—still a World Series record—including the cruellest one, a miscue in the ninth inning of the seventh game that handed Pittsburgh the victory. It's so very like baseball to bestow a record for defensive futility upon the man about whom Joe Sewell said, "I never saw anyone better with the glove."

Peck laboured for a few more years but, hampered by deteriorating legs, retired after the 1927 season. He then returned to Cleveland to manage for six seasons. Fired in 1933, he came back for a one-year stint in 1941. In all, the teams he steered won 500 games and lost 491.

He filled his offseasons much like Speaker did, with outdoor pursuits. As a young player in Cleveland, Peck was a member of the Cleveland Athletic Club, an organization whose members made frequent trips to Ontario in search of fish and game. They seem to have made contact with a guide from Marmora, Ontario, who entertained groups from Ohio. At some point no later than 1921, though probably earlier, Peckinpaugh regularly took part in these expeditions. The

*Marmora Herald* reported his presence, "hunting and fishing at Crowe Lake," which is just a mile or so west of the town of Marmora, along with New York second baseman Aaron Ward and Cleveland residents named Becker and Wright, in October 1921. Peck must have liked what he saw there, for he was soon the owner of a cabin on the lake, one to which he was said to return each offseason. Upon his death in 1977, his obituary in the *Cleveland Plain Dealer* noted that "[f]or years he spent a month in northern Canada with his family fishing for pike muskellunge." There exist photos of him with locals as late as 1934.

Similar 1923 ads in the *Examiner* and the *Marmora Herald* touted the appearance of Speaker's All-Stars and suggested that the exhibition was "a benefit game for the Marmora and Delora Branch G.W.V.A. Memorial Hall."

The Great War Veterans' Association was established in the wake of World War I, and amalgamated with other veterans groups in 1925 to form what's now called the Royal Canadian Legion, the activities of which include producing and selling Remembrance Day poppies each fall. In Marmora the service members' branch originally occupied a room in the municipal building that still stands at the corner of Highway 7 and Forsyth Street (it's now the public library and the Marmora Historical Society, where I undertook a portion of this research). Clearly the fundraising efforts were successful: they eventually built the hall in 1927, but quickly outgrew the building and in 1944 relocated, and relocated again in 1971, to Marmora's old school building, where Royal Canadian Legion Branch 237 remains today.

Did habitual offseason Marmora visitor Roger Peckinpaugh befriend members of the G.W.V.A. and pledge his help in fundraising for a new building? And did Peck present the organization to Spoke as a worthy beneficiary of proceeds when the latter was gathering volunteers for a Canadian expedition?

It might have all just been an excuse for a fishing trip, of course, but ballplayers in the 1920s didn't overlook opportunities to pad their income. This was the era of the reserve clause, a prevailing rule that allowed baseball's owners to prevent the movement of players, and which effectively resulted in a form of indentured servitude. Until Ruth became one of the biggest celebrities in the world and rewrote the rules, nobody was getting rich playing ball. It was by no means unusual for big-leaguers to go on these sorts of excursions in search of supplementary income during the fallow months. Some players worked regular jobs. Some traded on their names on Vaudeville stages. Others spent weeks on trains, in automobiles, aboard ships, and on the backs of mules, traipsing from town to town, putting on exhibitions in subpar facilities against whoever the town had mustered as opposition, divvying up the take, then sleeping in a lousy hotel or a guest bedroom or a chilly hayloft only to rise, catch the next train, and do it all over again.

Though Speaker was among the best-paid players in the game, his experience with Lannin and the Red Sox reinforced the precariousness of his situation. He, like all other ballplayers at the time, knew he had to scratch and claw for money just as he did for hits, outs, wins.

Promising a portion of the gate to a cause or local fund was often the price of doing business, so it's not inconceivable that Peckinpaugh's contacts in Marmora provided the auspices for the Saturday afternoon exhibition in Peterborough, a mutually beneficial arrangement for all involved.

--->>>|<<<---

Saturday, October 13, 1923 was cool but dry, a decent autumn afternoon for baseball at Riverside Park. The All-Stars had departed Rice Lake (not Toronto, as the *Examiner* had claimed) for Peterborough that morning. At some point that afternoon, likely before the game, Spoke paused to have his photo snapped on George Street. Cobb, meanwhile, apparently wished to get a jump on the outdoor fun and left the group shortly after the first exhibition at Scarboro for Temagami, well north of Peterborough, above Algonquin Park and accessible by rail.

In Peterborough, the Wellingtons—here to play the role of fodder for Spoke's men—took the field for what must have felt like a hopeless undertaking. Precise attendance figures are elusive, but the *Examiner* put the crowd in the thousands.

Saturday evening's paper contained an account that was exact in its portrayal of the facts of the game, but scant on expository detail, likely owing to a hard deadline; the paper didn't publish on Sundays, so anything written about the game would have to be printed the same day. The inning-by-inning breakdown gives us only the barest facts, and little colour.

Speaker, the record tells us, batted fifth. He tripled, knocking in a run, and later scored in the first inning. In the third, he flew out to centre, advancing Peckinpaugh from second to third. In the fifth, the most famous ballplayer ever to play in Peterborough singled past the shortstop, and scored. Finally, in the seventh, he hit his second triple of the game, and then came home on an error by the shortstop. His afternoon: 3 for 4 with a sacrifice, 2 RBIs, and 3 runs scored. Final: All-Stars 10, Wellingtons 3.

The men scattered after the game, released to their winter months to hunt, fish, or ride the train home. A few weeks later, back home in Cleveland, Speaker proposed to Mary Cudahy. They married in 1925. His batting stroke remained potent; in 1925 he hit .389, the highest average of his career. Spoke continued to play a solid centre field, and each season he added several dozen doubles to his total—he'd wind up with 792 for his career, a record then, and a record now.

In 1926 testimony emerged that Speaker and Cobb had conspired to fix a game in 1919, and that they'd placed bets with Cleveland's Smoky Joe Wood. Lefty pitcher Dutch Leonard, then a teammate of Cobb's in Detroit, claimed to have witnessed the transaction. Commissioner Kenesaw Mountain Landis took a dim view of such activities, but with Cobb's and Speaker's stature in mind he ruled quietly that they must resign their positions as player-managers of Detroit and Cleveland, respectively. When Leonard—who, it should be noted, had feuded with Cobb prior to 1919, when the former was with the Red Sox—declined to testify at a hearing, Judge Landis permitted the pair back into the game. Cobb wound up with Connie Mack's Philadelphia Athletics. Speaker signed with Washington, played a single season there, and then joined the Peach in Philly, where they both finished their big-league playing days in 1928. Speaker played only 64 games in his final season.

By a strange twist of fate, Cobb's last ever professional baseball game came in Toronto. By September, with the A's in a tight race with the Yankees, it was clear that Cobb's stamina was failing him. Mack, always eyeing the bottom line, continued to schedule off-day exhibition games, and agreed to one on September 18 in Toronto's brand new Maple Leaf Stadium against the building's namesake club. Cobb started the game in Toronto, though he hadn't started a game in weeks, had already recorded his 4,189th and final MLB hit (a pinch-hit double on September 3), and announced he'd be hanging 'em up at the end of the season. No doubt both he and Mack recognized that the gate would be better if he did.

-->>|<<--

I try not to be too bullish on it, but I'm always happy when my kids take an interest in playing sports, because I continue to hold tight to all the tropes about athletics contributing to a person's well-being, their physical and emotional development, and positive notions of civic engagement.

About three years after I began hunting down all the information I could on Speaker's and Cobb's Canadian adventures, just as Cormac was getting into basketball—developing a set shot, a chest pass, and a smooth layup—Theo began showing a real interest in playing baseball, one that wouldn't be satisfied by games of catch with his dad or siblings. He played a year of house league where his teammates' skill levels varied wildly. I don't want to overstate things lest I be accused of paternal favouritism, but it was hard not to conclude that he was the best player on that team. He played a lot of catcher in a set of borrowed equipment, which he enjoyed, and showed off a good right-handed bat. He learned how to pull his socks high and blouse his pants. He got a nickname ("Game Time," after the slogan on the T-shirt he'd worn to his first practice). Near the end of the season his coach recommended that Game Time try out for the competitive team.

When we'd throw the ball I couldn't help but notice the uptick in his velocity. He was bruising my palm, and he kept trying to throw breaking stuff, despite my soft protests about how it can mess up a young arm. When I told him I couldn't show him how to throw a slider, he checked a book on pitching and pitch grips out of the public library. He practised a curve, a slider, and would sometimes mess around with a sidearm delivery. For him, the idea that he could affect the path of the baseball just by altering the position of his fingers fell somewhere between physics and sorcery. He thought he could invent new pitches if he just experimented enough. I encouraged a knuckleball.

The tryouts were in September, after the house league season had wrapped up, and were held over several evenings. One of those tryouts, inevitably, was at the East City Bowl.

The would-be Peterborough Tigers scrimmaged. Theo was about the only kid present who hadn't been in the Tigers' program for years. He was green, a bit unformed, and didn't know the drills. But he could hit, and throw, and when they brought him in to pitch to a batter, he struck him out on five pitches.

My heart swelled watching it. I'd been dreading the blow to his psyche if he didn't make the team, but several nights later, sitting around the table playing cards with friends, we learned by email that he'd been added to the following season's Minor Mosquito Tier 2 team. The boys were in bed. It was after ten. But Christie saw the email come in, told me he'd made it. Theo, from upstairs, shouted, "I made it?!"

I get a tremulous feeling in my chest thinking about him there at the tryout in his grey baseball pants and high black socks, a black belt and a Blue Jays T-shirt, nine years old, wearing the West Michigan Whitecaps hat I'd bought him at that aforementioned game in Grand Rapids. A new glove on his hand, warming up with future teammates, tossing balls from right-centre to the first base line. The beginning of his organized baseball experience, on the same field where Tris Speaker and Roger Peckinpaugh and Les Nunamaker had played almost a century earlier. The Quaker Oats factory that Spoke would have seen looming over the grandstand roof is the same building that stands there now.

Legacies are complicated. The Otonabee glides through the heart of the city, literally and figuratively. Without it, Quaker would never have set up shop. The water has always drawn people to the spot, for transportation, for sustenance, for power. Peterborough-built canoes and boats have been used all over the world. The Otonabee's rapids made possible one of the earliest hydroelectric installations in Canada. Peterborough had electric streetlights before any other locale in the country, and the cheap, reliable electricity drew Thomas Edison to build his first facility outside the US there in 1891. You can't discuss the history of this town without dealing with the good and the ill of Canadian General Electric. CGE provided stable middle-class jobs for generations while polluting both local land and bodies. For decades workers in Peterborough breathed, handled, and absorbed toxic substances, insulated their homes with surplus asbestos, and in the end GE upped and left, leaving behind cancer, respiratory illness, and a huge patch of unusable land and buildings sliding into ruin, right in the middle of town. There were six thousand employees at the operation's zenith, until it succumbed to the same forces draining manufacturing jobs from towns and cities all over the US and Canada.

Spoke and his peers played before stands packed with CGE workers, Quaker employees, people who built canoes, who tended the turbines. It's fitting that the ballpark sits on the banks of the river—there'd be no crowd, and no town, without the Otonabee.

As a resident of this city, and as a participant in its sporting life, I'm connected materially to all of it. To manufacturing, to unions, to the life of this city, and to men in spikes, in flannels, playing in the World Series, riding overnight trains from Washington to New York, sleeping with their hats over their faces. How proximate this all is, how real.

My mother was born in Pictou, Nova Scotia, where Ruth stopped in at the Lobster Carnival in 1936, and they presented him with a mounted sixteen pounder. In nearby Westville, where the Miners of the Central Baseball League were hosting Liverpool, he interrupted the game to take a few swings, smacking one or twenty balls over the fence, depending on who you ask.

It's just a fact of the way things were. Ballplayers were itinerant, desperate for money, and went wherever there was a buck to be made. I'm sure a thousand similar stories lie in old newspapers and faded photos, in diminishing memories and anecdotes, from Cape Breton to Calexico. But this one's ours, and I'll keep mentioning it to anyone in earshot as long as I've got the lungs to do so.

Life gives you everything and then takes it away. This is the sweet in-between, the very middle, and I'm doing all I can to enjoy it. The warm air, the grass, my boy in cleats, history, hope, the firmness of the bleachers beneath me. The *con-*

*nection* of it all; in a dozen years of living in this town, noth-ing—not the boys' birth, not launching a few books here, not birthday parties or graduations—has made me feel more like I finally have an answer to the question *Where are you from*?

In 1923 the East City Bowl had a different orientation, rotated ninety degrees counterclockwise from its current position, so that home plate was in what's now right field, and the diamond was flanked by two covered wooden grand-stands. But it's also the same field, the same soil, shaded by the same trees. Generations of local kids have suited up and tried out here, made the team or not, played on the riverbank while parents and friends, neighbours and strangers, sat shoulder to shoulder in the stands and cheered.

# RELICS

In summer's deep groove—long, pollen-rich days, warm nights, white bulbs on a string hung from the porch to a nearby sycamore—Christie, the kids, and I temporarily relocated to the Catskills, a farmhouse on forty-two fragrant acres of just-cut hay, brambly hedgerows, and wild green hills. The view from the porch: a half-dozen outbuildings in the process of being swallowed by the flora, a century-old hydrangea vibrating with the energy of hundreds of buzzing insects, and those gently rolling hills.

The view was entirely concordant with the old myth that baseball had been invented in a field not terribly far away by a young man named Doubleday who'd later go on to perform feats of Civil War heroism. There's no truth to that story, but the scene from a porch in the Catskills—achingly still, out of time, lush, and abundant—lured me into *wanting* the story to be true.

One evening I scanned the radio dial. I couldn't get the Yankees' signal, though I did briefly find a Nationals game. I located, and then lost, the Mets. The crickets trilled as static washed out the announcers' call.

We drove into Scranton and took in a rain-delayed and -shortened minor league game. Flash flooding, a state of emergency declared, Shane Victorino—the Flyin' Hawaiian—rendered in a life-sized bobblehead on the concourse. We returned with ballcaps, pocket schedules, a program, the plastic batting helmet in which our nachos were served. When the vacation was over we headed home and added these things to the trove, the cache of items garnered from lives lived alongside baseball, and in time these artifacts will take on the gravity of relics.

--->>><<<---

It happens from time to time that someone somewhere unearths a lost piece of baseball's history—a document, a scrap, a testament of witness. Such was the case in 2018 when a Boston man rescued from the back of a drawer good-quality colour footage of Ted Williams's last game, an afternoon match from September 1960. There were few fans in attendance that day at Fenway Park, but among them was John Updike, whose missive from the event, published in *The New Yorker*, has consistently garnered praise as a supreme example of the art of writing sports.

These discoveries of physical proof of the earthly lives of the saints illuminate the collective history of the game. But there's another category of the game's ephemera to consider: the tokens of personal history, the items that chronicle our individual experiences. Tickets stubs and snapshots, the first cap you owned and subsequently wore out, partially filled-out scorecards.

Of Ichiro, I have ticket stubs, photos, cards, a jersey. Most treasured of all, though, is the Mariners cap I bought at Safeco Field during his rookie season. I remember thinking I'd paid too much for it—the exchange rate was killing us that summer—but I've been wearing it for twenty years, so I guess it was worth it. To anyone else it's a faded, shapeless Mariners cap, but for me it's a remnant of the first time I saw Ichiro, and all of the things I have watched him do since.

Beyond Ichiro, I have a room full of items commemorating other players and teams. Dozens of ballcaps (they're my greatest weakness), thousands of cards, souvenir programs, shirts, bobbleheads, rally towels, and on and on. This, I suppose, is my collection, though the word collect suggests to me purposefully buying. *Accrue* feels more accurate—found, discovered at thrift stores, rescued from deep closets, received via stadium giveaways on nights we have been fortunate to attend.

I want to say that baseball is unique in the richness of artifacts if offers, though I can't quantify that. I might be seeing that only through the lens of my own life. From the time that baseball first became a hot, holy belief system for me, I have hoarded cards, shirts, bits of paper, old pieces of equipment. Anything bearing a team's logo, a depiction of a batter or fielder, or the places where the game is played.

By virtue of its age, its place in the culture, and the timing of its zenith alongside the postwar rise of consumerism, baseball offers a wealth of material unmatched by other sporting pursuits. And even the most generic, cheaply produced, sponsor-adorned example of it catches my interest. I'm a sucker for all of it.

➤➤❮❮❮

Once, a trip to a Peterborough thrift store offered up a Gary Carter Expos jersey that fit Christie like it was made for her. For me there was a catcher's mitt, worn but sturdy, with Randy Hundley's signature reproduced along the thick, pinky-side pad. Hundley was the Cubs' regular backstop for a number of years, including the ill-fated '69 team that held a comfortable lead in the standings before a black cat appeared out of nowhere at Shea Stadium and crossed Ron Santo's path as he stood in the on-deck circle. Thereafter the Cubs were overtaken by the Miracle Mets, who went on to win the Series.

I'd always wanted a catcher's mitt and this one cost me thirteen bucks. It needed a small bit of re-lacing, which I did with amateurish skill and enthusiasm. The day after I bought it, it featured prominently in a day of catch, shagging flies, a chip truck, cold Cokes, a bag of cherries. There was a stinging grounder and a bloody nose, and later there was swimming.

We played ball in the Catskills with that glove, and my childhood Andre Dawson outfielder's mitt (also repaired), and the kids' gloves, a mix of hand-me-downs and newer models. We had a pair of Louisville Sluggers and an assortment of balls. And we had all kinds of space.

Theo was trying to learn to spit, which I had to officially discourage, though it is also true that I did the same thing as a boy of his age. Adelaide had a wicked arm she wanted to show off in her little brothers' presence. The boys were eager to learn the jargon, to absorb baseball's mannerisms. They were all hungry for stories of heroics and victory, failure and misery.

The three of them were dressed as follows: shorts, running shoes, dirty ballcaps, and T-shirts with baseball logos on them. I was dressed identically. These summers with my kids allow me to revert to a kind of boyhood—my wardrobe is basically identical to my pre-adolescent summers, as is my rabid interest in the ongoing pennant races. It's also likely that I'd be this way regardless of having children.

But as it is, I have playmates. I dropped a half-dozen balls on the ground and paced off thirty steps, turned, crouched, and held up my left hand with the Hundley glove on it. "Gimme your best pitches," I told them. Cormac attempted a funky grip and the ball sailed from his fingers, high and ten feet to my left. "That was my curve," he said. He picked up another ball and repeated the motion, sending this one squarely into my palm.

I could count on my hand the number of these warm, easeful days we'd have, though I know it looked different to them. I remember that feeling of summer laid out before me like an endlessly unrolling carpet. And if I had to guess at the source of the appeal of all those pieces of baseball memorabilia I've accumulated, as well as those I've yet to acquire, I'd say that it lies in having realized, at a date I cannot now pinpoint, that such an abundance of time is illusory. That the supply of hot afternoons and inky dusks, of sunburned and fly-bitten hours spent with caps on our heads and gloves on our hands, is limited. The souvenirs, scorecards, and pieces of equipment are material acknowledgements of that, objects to keep in lieu of being able to hold tight to moments we've felt slip, or failed to notice at all as they occurred. They're small monuments to the way life felt before we realized just how short all this is.

# JUNIOR, AND THE WAY
# THINGS WERE

It's hard now, at this remove, to convey the impact Ken Griffey Jr. had upon the landscape when he landed in 1989, a nineteen-year-old phenom with a championship pedigree, a megawatt smile, and pure, unfiltered athletic ability that rendered baseball fans positively giddy. With his cap turned backwards in an unaffected display of comfort in a big-league ballpark, Junior was the youthful and exuberant antidote to the sourness of the concurrently unfolding Pete Rose situation; in August of Junior's rookie season, Rose was banned for life from baseball for betting on games involving the team he managed. It was a scandal for MLB, but Junior was the jolt of positivity fans needed to get past it.

The stadium was his living room, we understood, the natural habitat of a young man raised in ballparks, watching his dad win consecutive World Series as a member of the Big Red Machine. It was impossible to watch Junior and not like what you saw; it was just as hard not to wish you were him.

He offered something that seemed to fit the times, the last piece of the puzzle of the dynamic and post-racial future we'd been promised, a beacon in a way that few athletes ever prove to be. The Berlin Wall fell and Griffey stood in centre field. Everything, it was plain to see, was right with the world. He was emblematic of a dazzling confidence that told a generation of brightly clothed kids that not only could they hit home runs, but they'd also feed the world, save the environment, say no to drugs, ban the bomb, and end racism. He was an animated PSA. He was optimism in human form.

The feeling carried over into the '90s, and The Kid kept going, tattooing baseballs, climbing outfield walls, smiling his way through interviews and All-Star Game introductions. He was a five-tool player, but everything you needed to know about his game was in that swing. It was at once smooth and powerful. If you wanted to affirm a belief in heaven, that swing was all you required; the motion's provenance was clear. It was archetypal, a natural marriage of grace and power, something rare and intoxicating.

The Gold Gloves piled up—there'd be ten in all. His defense was an extension of his churning exuberance. The same swift engine that powered his swing allowed him to chase down balls in the outfield and drove him around the bases. When he rounded third at a gallop in the eleventh inning of the deciding game of the '95 ALDS against the Yankees, set free from first by an Edgar Martínez double, there seemed no point in doubting that he'd wind up safe at home.

But he was most revered as a hitter, riding that matchless swing into the homer-happy zaniness of the late '90s. He emerged from that tainted era unsullied by suspicion. We might lament the fact that his habit of mashing fifty-odd taters a year put him shy of the history-baiting performances of McGuire and Sosa and, later, Bonds. We could bemoan the manner in which his grace was out-glittered in the midst of the gonzo atmosphere of those post-strike, pre-millennial seasons. Or we might just appreciate what we had when Junior was on our TVs piloting balls over walls with that smile on his face.

Then he left Seattle. Long before LeBron acted on a similar desire to return to Ohio, Ken Griffey Jr. decided he wanted to go home, and so was granted a trade to the Reds. That was the start of the end. The decline was abrupt, and then went on far too long, though when he unloosed that swing it was tempting for everyone, including him, to believe he could go on doing it indefinitely. But following his first full year in Cincinnati, which featured respectable stats, the numbers fell off precipitously, and more alarming to us as we watched was the eye test: it was so glaringly clear that he wasn't what he'd been. The body had begun to fail him, as it will all of us. It was his legs, mostly, and without them he could not stand nearly so tall as he had—neither in the field, nor in our collective estimation.

There were yet highlights to come, mostly of the milestone variety, such as when he hit his 500th home run on Father's Day in 2004, with Ken Sr. in attendance. But he was coasting then, mostly, on what he'd already done, and the remnants of that dazzling natural ability still visible in tantalizing glimpses. There was a forgotten half-season with the White Sox, and then a return to Seattle to serve primarily as a figurehead to a franchise and a city still in the thrall of what he'd once been.

The end, in June 2010, was sudden and not wholly dignified, but by no means premature. It would have been better if things had lined up to afford him a victory tour like the one David Ortiz was able to take, but sometimes endings just happen.

Having settled into a comfortable retirement, The Kid was ushered into Cooperstown on his first ballot in 2016, in a near-unanimous affirmation of his greatness.

Among his many admirers was a young Ichiro Suzuki. Ichiro has called Junior "my favourite superstar," and the two sat down for an awkward meeting in 1995, when Ichiro was a bright and spindly twenty-two year old and Griffey was firmly the best baseball player in the world. With a Japanese camera crew in tow, Ichiro travelled to the Griffeys' home in Cincinnati and met with Kens Junior and Senior, as well as an interpreter, for an endearingly staged conversation. Ichiro—in the middle of his run of three straight Japanese Pacific League MVP seasons—looked doubly diminutive for his naturally wiry frame and the prevailing clothing styles. The Griffeys played it cool, appearing genuinely happy to meet the newly minted Japanese superstar, though not entirely sure just what all the fuss was about. Junior gifted Ichiro an autographed bat, and given Ichiro's reverence for the game's history, and for his heroes, it's safe to assume he still possesses that lumber.

By the time Ichiro joined the Mariners, Junior was entering his second year as a Red. The two wouldn't be teammates until eight years later, when Griffey ended up back in Seattle for his last lap. They spent a season and a half touring their mutual admiration around the American League, until finally Griffey reached the end of his time.

It's tempting to imagine what might have been had Junior stuck around the Pacific Northwest; would those 2001 Mariners, with their 116 victories, have overcome the Yankees in the American League Championship Series? Maybe beaten the Diamondbacks for that year's title?

Probably not. Baseball's math doesn't usually favour such simple addition. But what-ifs are the second-favourite pastime of all baseball fans. Griffey's career, for all the big numbers and the prestige of the names he passed in record books, will always be something of a what-if. Would a healthy Kid have bested Hank Aaron's home run total? Would he have won a World Series?

In the end, it doesn't really matter, and we have to let go of the what-ifs. What he did was beautiful to watch, and we were fortunate to have been there to do the watching.

# ICHIRO RUNS
# THE NUMBERS DOWN

After his first stint with the Mariners, Ichiro drifted. Traded to the Yankees in July of 2012 while the Bombers visited Seattle, he simply switched clubhouses and suited up in New York's road greys. Batting eighth, he patiently endured a lengthy ovation from the Mariner crowd, then rapped a single and stole second base. He was primarily a fourth outfielder for his new team, helping the first-place Yanks ground the Orioles in the Division Series before being swept by Detroit in the AL Championship Series. He re-signed with New York for 2013 and '14, when injuries allowed him to fill in at all three out-field spots, as well as at DH. Neither of those Yankee teams made the playoffs, and when his two-year deal expired, he was cut loose.

Before spring training in 2015, he signed with the Miami Marlins, who already boasted a starting outfield of Marcell Ozuna and future MVPs Christian Yelich and Giancarlo Stanton. It seemed unlikely that Ichiro would see much action, but injuries again intervened; he played over 130 games for Miami in each of the next three seasons.

In 2016, in the ninth inning of a mid-June getaway matinee at San Diego, the stands half-empty, Ichiro stepped up and rapped a double down the right-field line, moving Giancarlo Stanton to third. Ichiro stood on second base, the sudden holder of another record, albeit an unofficial one: his 4,257th professional base hit—combined from the NPB and MLB—moved him past Pete Rose in career knocks.

Grey-haired, a bit weathered, but otherwise appearing for all the world like the same limber, catlike enigma he was when he notched number one, the Marlins' outfielder/interleague DH/bench player doffed his batting helmet and nodded with the same hint of solemnity and apparent desire to return to business that he's displayed with every record he's broken. And there have been many.

You're welcome to split hairs all you like, cling to the go-go, vial-in-pocket exuberance of Charlie Hustle's heyday and say, as Rose cantankerously did, that Ichiro's great and all but he sure as hell isn't the all-time hit leader because he collected his first 1,278 in Japan which, sorry, ain't no major league. We can have that debate, if you're dead set on digging your heels in. Or we can say that they're different accomplishments, and agree that the only loser in this scenario is the already besmirched respectability of Rose, who spent decades clutching with death-like desperation at the remaining tatters of his relevance.

Meanwhile, Ichiro remained an elegant figure amid inelegant times, quiet, rigorous, determined to the point of doggedness. Watching him over the years, it was apparent that, whether or not he possessed any more English than he was willing to publicly let on, he wasn't one to use language superfluously anyway. He would rather just do his job.

He began that job in 1992, played nine seasons, and then relocated to Seattle in 2001. The world was different then, if only by a million disparate increments, recognizable at this present-day remove but subjectively alien to us in its lack of concerns. The twin towers still stood, the War on Terror hadn't begun to lurch into aimless, destructive motion, and the second President Bush was mostly just a punchline. The air we breathed had yet to be seeded with the paranoid existential dread to which we've all become accustomed. All of that makes it even more beautiful to remember what Ichiro did that summer, rubbing it squarely in the creased, leathery faces of those who were certain that the brilliance he displayed in the NPB simply wouldn't translate. It did, for the better part of two decades.

Longevity is crucial in the quest for a record like career base hits. Like Rose (1963–1986), like Cobb (1905–1928), you don't rack up over 4,000 hits without logging the time. But time alone is not enough. The key is consistency across the years, a machine-like replication of excellence, the repetition of all the little things beyond endurance to the point of complete absurdity. Up to that afternoon in San Diego, Ichiro's Major League hit total included 113 home runs, 91 triples, and 346 doubles—like the one that put him past Rose. But the overwhelming majority of his hits, going back even to his days in Japan, looked a lot like his first-inning single, the one that tied him for the record—Ichiro, possessed of a spindliness that belied his strength, slapping at the ball to have it dribble across the infield grass while he scampered safely through the bag at first. He did that reliably, over and over again, longer than the Florida/Miami Marlins had been in existence. In sizing up the sheer scale of his accomplishment, cold numbers fall short; it takes a wide lens to appreciate the stoic perfection day after day, year after year.

The vagaries and ambiguities of statistical comparison have allowed some to claim that Maris didn't actually best Ruth, and that Nolan Ryan can't fairly be compared to Cy Young or Walter Johnson. They've also been invoked in the case of Ichiro's hit total. The numbers don't lie, except when they do. That's fine. We can make up a new name for the record, or hang an asterisk on it. This is the beauty of all of baseball's imprecision, that sweet spot where cold calculation meets historical subjectivity and human sloppiness. We might call Rose the Major League record-holder and Ichiro the Global Hit King. We can twist and explain, engage in semantics, drill down into the granular nubs of both sides of the argument, and still not arrive at anything resembling a consensus. I doubt Ichiro ever cared. He seemed wholly unconcerned with how he might be used as a cipher for the broader arguments of others. He was too busy worrying about what he might control, namely hitting a baseball, putting his head down, and charging out of the box, running to beat the devil.

# SIMULACRA

Central among my beliefs is that the 1987 Topps set is the
finest collection of baseball cards ever produced. There
are no hard facts to support this claim, only my personal
zealotry, and though I understand that my love is highly
subjective, and the product of timing and circumstance as
much as it is of appealing design, I'm unshakable: this is the
set, this is the year.

Arguments can and frequently are made for the 1952 Topps
set—with its bold primary colours, its painterly portraits, and
its Mickey Mantle rookie card—and had I been born a generation earlier I'd likely agree. If I'd been alive to see it first, I'd
have been aware that the 1987s owed much to the 1962 set, and
so might've fallen in love with that one to the exclusion of all
others. On the other hand, the 1915 Cracker Jack set is iconic
for good reason, and our impressions of the white border tobacco card set issued from 1909 to 1911 are necessarily favour-
able both for the design's simplicity as well as for its inclusion of
the famed Honus Wagner card. But give me 1987.

Each card presents a photo, either action or posed, with
the team's logo in a roundel in the upper-left corner, and
the player's name in a coloured rectangular box with a black
border in the lower right, the name rendered in an all-caps
font that appears to be a kissing cousin to comic sans. But the
background is what distinguishes the set: faux wood, the un-
stained grain of a Louisville Slugger running top to bottom,
with enough subtle variance from card to card to suggest
that real wood was used, or at least consulted, at some point
during the design process. The overall effect places the cards
adjacent to something real, something natural: wood bats
swung through thick summer air, connecting with genuine
horsehide balls, which are sent skidding across dirt and grass
before settling into the soft, worn pockets of leather mitts.

Career stats—often including minor league numbers, if the player in question has only a year or two of big league experience, and so speaking offhandedly of Kinston, North Carolina, or Syracuse, New York, or Visalia, California—are listed on the reverse in blue against a highlighter-yellow background, overtop an unbleached cardboard stock.

Beautiful.

In Canada they were branded O-Pee-Chee, and featured what felt like a token effort toward bilingualism, the player's position and small biographical fun facts in both French and English, and yet with statistical categories listed only in English. They were otherwise virtually identical to the American originals.

I bought them from convenience stores—Becker's on Youville Drive, or Mac's on St. Joseph Boulevard, in Ottawa—for thirty-five cents for a wax pack of seven cards. If my father was sent out in the evening for a litre of milk, sometimes he'd come home with one in hand. My friends collected them too, and we traded with an eye toward amassing our favourites. We were not yet victims of the belief that these rectangles of paper would make us rich. This was a couple years before the hobby became an industry, at least in my part of the world, characterized by conventions and trade shows where children were elbowed aside by grown men with dollar signs where their eyes ought to have been. The card and comic shop down the hill on St. Joseph hadn't yet opened.

Joe Posnanski has said that baseball is never as beautiful as it is when you're ten years old. I guess I'm testifying to that—or anyway, to that general time in my life between about eight and twelve. I watched the NBC *Game of the Week*, scattered Blue Jays games on CBC, TSN, and CTV, and a weekly digest show on CTV called *Blue Jays Banter*. When a Jays game wasn't on TV, which was the norm, I listened to the broadcast on AM radio, CFRA or W1310, on a transistor unit next to my bed.

Around the time that the Blue Jays reported to Dunedin for spring training in 1987, I would have started collecting the cards in question, noticing with great interest when the display box appeared on store counters. This was mere months after Boston's historic Game Six collapse ("It gets through Buckner!") and the Mets' subsequent title; it was two seasons after 1985's painful memories, which saw Toronto enter the postseason for the first time in their existence, only to lose the ALCS in heartbreaking fashion to the Royals (I have yet to forgive George Brett). Kansas City then defeated their cross-state rivals, the Cardinals, in seven games to earn their first title. Stacked together, along with what would eventually transpire at the end of the '87 season—Frank Viola and the Twins besting the Cardinals to win their first Series—this might represent the most thrilling three-year run in the game's history, with three consecutive seven-gamers that'd be hard to imagine if they hadn't actually happened. It was, I mean to say, a wonderful time to be a baseball-loving kid, and a great time to collect cards.

›››‹‹‹

We'd lived on Rivermill Crescent in suburban Ottawa since the late summer of 1984, when we'd arrived to find our newly built house surrounded by mounds of dirt, open foundations, and unpaved driveways. Across the street, behind the houses under construction, was a great thick forest, a ravine treed with mostly deciduous species—beech and birch and maple—and hatched with trails. In the middle of it wended a silty creek cut deep into banks of mud.

As the neighbourhood rose around us, the houses filled with families who presented a tribute to the nascent diversity of Canada's capital. My new friends' families came from Hong Kong and Pakistan; the boys my age were first-generation kids who loved Michael Jordan and the Teenage Mutant Ninja Turtles.

My friend Wil lived across the street. He was a Giants fan—Will Clark, Kevin Mitchell—though what it meant to be a fan of a team on the West Coast, or really of a team from anywhere other than the nearest major market, was not what it means today. Before the internet the scarcity of information, the lack of regular televised games, and the lag between when a thing happened and when it appeared in the newspaper's sports section all conspired to illustrate how far away everything was on this enormous continent. Chicago was the moon; San Francisco, and all the West Coast, was Mars. You saw those players in colour on rare *Game of the Week* appearances and then during the playoffs, if you were lucky; otherwise you contented yourself with deciphering box scores, cutting their photos out of glossy magazines, and collecting their cards.

As I preoccupied myself with all this, my older brother and sister wandered the thickets of adolescence, almost completely obscured from my view. Peter is six years older than I am, Robyn seven. For a long time the differences in our ages meant we had very little to do with one another. I sat alone in the backseat on family road trips while Robyn and Peter stayed home and hung out with friends, threw parties, waded neck-deep into teenage dramas.

Robyn had a boyfriend from across the Ottawa River named Yvon. He was dark-haired, stubbly, smoked cigarettes, and spoke with a Québécois accent. He was always kind to me. Took me fishing once. Yvon drove a 1976 Dodge Colt in a swampy shade of green that had originally been my grandmother's; it came into my parents' possession and they then sold it to Yvon for a few hundred dollars. I remember him paying my father cash, handing over what was to that point the largest sum of money I'd ever seen in my life, thinking that this was the adult world. This was what it was to transact business, to be connected to commerce.

Yvon didn't know baseball, but he treated me like something other than a child, by which I mean he listened to me with patience. On a night in late summer or early fall, he parked the Colt between the street lights on Rivermill, across from the forest, and we lay atop the hood watching the Aurora play across the face of the night. It was astonishing, but what should have made the heavens feel proximate instead made me aware of the terrifying size of the sky under which we huddled.

⤞⥊⥊⇤

I had thought, until quite recently, that I had a complete set of the 1987 O-Pee-Chees, but if I ever did I don't now. The whole set comprises almost 400 cards; I might have half of that. My stack seemed so large to my young eyes, but now it looks small. This, I take it, is an example of how things from that point in our lives come to assume outsized proportions. We build our own legends and then accept them as facts.

There are complete sets kicking around on eBay, on Amazon, and it's tempting to go all in, to fork over a relatively small sum in order to capture in adulthood what tantalized and inspired wonder in childhood. But it wouldn't be the same. Something about this set tells me I could never actually complete it, not in the most important sense. Maybe the trick, or the lesson, is to be happy with what I already have.

There are cards in this set that I can sketch with my eyes closed, so iconic are they for me, so emblematic of that time. Some are in fact what flashes into my mind when a name is mentioned.

Texas catcher Darrell Porter in a pair of ridiculously large eyeglasses that may or may not be back in style now, depending on when you're reading this.

Jack Morris, in Detroit's home whites, having just released a pitch, his limbs in unnatural degrees of torque, his face a grimace of effort.

Fernando Valenzuela, fresh off a 21-win campaign, in Dodger roads, his plant leg rigid as he lunges forward to send

a screwball toward whatever unfortunate National Leaguer
has dug in sixty and one-half feet away.

The Giants' Juan Berenguer, a workhorse righty, looking
imperiously over his left shoulder, above the camera, beyond
the photographer, toward the horizon.

The luxuriously mustachioed Keith Hernandez, recent
World Series champion, looking light and pleased with life,
on a practice field somewhere in Florida.

Sturdy Floyd Bannister in the White Sox' beach blanket
home uniforms, his shoulders wide, his right leg just slightly
recessed at the beginning of his motion.

Marty Barrett, the Boston second baseman, whose name
in Vin Scully's mouth during that 1986 Series is a sound in-
delibly linked to my childhood—Mah-ahty Bawrhit, Scully
sang/spoke, inserting diphthongs and pauses where most
of us wouldn't dream of putting them—and whose '87 card
depicts him in bright sunshine acting as the pivot in a double
play in what can only be spring training, for why else would
there be a basketball hoop immediately beyond the wall just
barely visible over Barrett's shoulder?

A trio of A's captured by a photographer during the same
road game, in Tiger Stadium, I think, wearing Oakland's 1986
green tops, and bathed in similar light: glowering Dave Stew-
art, in his windup, staring holes through a hitter, who is out
of frame; reliever and possessor of an all-time great baseball
name, Moose Haas, warming up along the first base side,
the rows of seats beyond him out of focus, receding into the
darkness of the ballpark's overhang; and still-skinny Mark
McGwire, depicted during his '86 cup of coffee, with no way
of knowing all that lay before him.

Dave Stieb looking so uncannily like an old gym teacher of
mine—same winged haircut, same mustache—who used to
lead us in laps around the gym, playing Beach Boys records
on a portable turntable perched on the gym's stage, and who
would reward us at the end of class by walking on his hands

around the middle of the floor, finally flopping back down, his face red and bulging.

Ernie Whitt, the avuncular and soft-seeming catcher, whose name still causes my father to reminisce over one of Whitt's late-career stolen bases, an event so implausible it warranted a headline in the next day's write-up, or so recalls my father.

Willie Upshaw who, with apologies to Fred McGriff and, later, John Olerud—and even Carlos Delgado—remains my favourite Jays first-sacker, for reasons that are spongy and un-scientific, but that owe much to this very card, with Upshaw's pose of readiness, crouched, that huge trapper open and wait-ing near his right knee, the lingering scent of bubblegum still borne by the cardboard.

A shoebox full of these, many more forming untidy stacks on my desk and office bookshelf. Still others used as book-marks. The Marty Barrett card pinned to the wall above my workspace.

Looking over them all now, deep in the pre-opening day trough of winter, interspersed with other baseball cards that span a forty-year period, what first strikes me is how unique the '87s are. Shuffle together a deck of assorted cards—O-Pee-Chees or Topps from 1979, or 1983, with some from 2003, or 2013, and some Bowman cards from any given year, a hand-ful of Upper Decks from the early nineties, a few Donruss, a Leaf or two—and then rifle through the stack.

Most every card is bordered in white, but the '87s, with their wood grain, stand out immediately. They're unlike any other issue from Topps, or any other manufacturer of the period. It's not evocative of natural materials; rather what I see is how the wood grain is perfectly in tune with the era's penchant for simulacra. That faux-wood border, veneered furniture, wood panelling, canned sitcom laughter, drum machines, artificial turf—all *suggestive* of something real, but in their deficiencies creating further space between the manufactured and the real. I see not the proximity to realness, but the distance between the actual and the representational. I see the desire to simulate, to contain, to miniaturize. I see the need to recreate something random and unruly using something inexpensive, convenient, safe.

→→⟩⟨⟨←

When we weren't collecting, trading, or memorizing baseball cards, or playing road hockey, G.I. Joe, or DOS-based video games in Wil's unfinished basement, we were in the forest. We played war there, hiding behind trunks, laying down amid the ferns, using sticks as machine guns. We rode our bikes on some of the trails. We caught frogs and threw rocks into the creek. Gradually, we pushed at the borders of what we knew of the forest, pressing further and further into it, adding clearings and swales to our mental maps, wondering what still lay beyond.

We'd heard of some kids who'd found cattle bones in our woods, and others who'd pushed all the way through to Orleans Boulevard—the edge of the known world. There was a sandpit, somebody told us, where teenagers rode dirtbikes and held bush parties.

Wil and I found a fence one day, or the remains of one. A farmer's partition, toppled, regularly spaced logs slumping out of their ancient post holes, and strung with rusted barbed wire. I had trouble incorporating this into my understanding of time and space, this echo of a time removed from 1987, the suggestion of a world beyond my own.

Above, nailed to a tree, a sign: NO TRESPASSING, it beckoned.

# OVERRUNNING IT

Late February on the Space Coast is a good time and place to duck out of the cold Ontario weather and soak in a bit of sunshine along with the deep Floridian weirdness. Take the kids to see the rockets at Kennedy, sit in a low chair on a brown sugar beach and get gradually day-sozzled on Guatemalan beer, or duck into Moe's Lounge in New Smyrna Beach to drink two-dollar Lites and watch televised golf with the local retirees. Then maybe head over to the State Park near Orange City to rent a canoe and paddle gator-infested waters, strafed by black vultures and large, fictional-looking birds, for the chance to see some manatees, large and stationary in the gentle river current.

When that fun's all used up, you might as well make the drive into the Greater Orlando region to take in a spring training game.

Christie, the kids and I did just that, on a day that threatened to dump rain onto the vast paved expanses and prehistoric vegetal tangle of Lake Buena Vista. We filed through the turnstiles at Champion Stadium, site of the game between the Mets and the Atlantas. The afternoon was mellow in all the right ways, and things broke in our favour: the parking was free, the rain held off, the saxophone quartet absolutely nailed "Take Me Out to the Ballgame," and a kindly usher handed us a retrieved foul ball on our way out.

In the ninth inning, a rail-thin infielder, whose name I forgot the moment I learned it, stepped up for New York, who were down two runs. He stung a line drive up the middle. The likewise nameless player occupying centre for Atlanta raced in, and you could tell he was thinking, "This is my chance! Here's where I do something amazing and make the brass take notice!" Only he'd broken too early, and he realized it too late. Despite his leaping attempt to spear it, the ball sailed over his head. By this time, the batter was cruising toward second. The centre fielder knew he'd blown it, that all he could do was watch the ball skitter clear to the wall and hope his right fielder could heave it back to the infield in time to limit the damage to a triple.

When the runner rounded third, I placed my hands on my head in an unconscious gesture of disbelief. The throw reached the catcher a split second after the runner slid in, head first, dust flying, safe as Fort Knox. An inside-the-park homer.

I was cheering for the Mets, because of old grievances (I have not forgiven Atlanta for flying the Canadian flag upside down before Game Two of the 1992 World Series), and because you can't cheer for a team whose name you refuse to say. And I was genuinely thrilled to see an inside-the-parker for the first time in my life.

I was also overjoyed that the kids got to witness it. My reign as curator of their worlds is winding down. Where baseball is concerned, they remain soft targets, but the clock's ticking on that too, especially where the nearly teenaged girl is concerned.

So if I was overly enthusiastic about a sloppy play in a spring training game, my excitement was genuine. And yet for all my cheering, I felt the greatest sense of connection with that centre fielder, walking out to his position with his back to the plate even while the ump signalled "safe," recognizing that he'd fucked up, and trying hard to figure out how he was going to erase that boner in the minds of the coaches before he was shipped down to the Gwinnett Stripers, or back to the Single-A squad in Rome, Mississippi, to fart away another season.

Every writer's got to hone an angle, the thing that's unmistakably theirs. Or, to steal from Richard Ford, to find and write about that thing which causes a commotion in the heart. I have just betrayed mine. I cheer for the runner rounding third and chugging into home, but I *identify* with the guy who overran the ball.

Because Lord knows I've overrun a few balls. I've taken my shot only to realize my aim is off, my gut instincts have led me astray. I've felt that pang of sudden terror while recognizing the ball is about to sail over my head and there's not a thing I can do to minimize the damage.

This is metaphorical, you understand. The instances in question have had to do with books, and writing, the stuff I broadly identify as "the work." I've brazenly introduced myself to heroes by misquoting their words, sent awkward and fawning emails to people whose work I've admired. I've made too-confident pitches. I've read truly shitty pieces aloud in public.

After the terror has passed, and the regret has lost its initial sting, each time I've been glad I took my shot. These failures are interesting because without a thousand of them, that slim moment of victory wouldn't mean a damn thing. The careful and considered—the daily, repetitious work—builds us into the people we are, establishes the skills and the techniques that might one day bring success. Occasional overrunning is a way to see where you stand, to measure yourself against your own expectations and those of the world. The trial and error of self-definition. It can be embarrassing, and chastening, and damaging to the ego, but ultimately, it contributes to the development of the knotty, fibrous hide required to survive the act of putting yourself out there.

That centre fielder's name was Isranel Wilson, by the way. He goes by Izzy. He was then twenty years old, from Saint Maarten, signed by Atlanta in 2014. He's bounced around in the low minors since then—the Gulf Coast League, the Appalachian League—and his role here is to stand in for all of us, because in his miscalculation of the ball's trajectory and his hasty decision to sprint toward the infield, he transcended his position as a late-inning substitution in the most meaningless of all baseball games and became an emblem. He's me, he's you, on what we *hope* are our best days, charging in, oversure and underprepared, damn the torpedoes, putting all the likely consequences out of our minds for a moment, taking our best shot, even if history tells us that some measure of caution is in order. Suspecting it might be the last shot we get, we're gonna charge forward, even as we fear that in the very next heartbeat it will prove to be something from which we will be forced to learn.

# TIMELINES

On the first timeline I am forty-something years old, a husband, father of three children, builder of things, writer of things, breaker and fixer of things, maker of mistakes, possessor of a desire to whittle down, slough away, simplify, to realize a slenderness of being. I have a left knee that occasionally balks, and a left wrist that aches in the cold. I want to be pliant, open, but I can't tell if I'm hardening or going soft. I am forgetful, but try to remember to make things right, day in and day out. This is my own timeline; private, enclosed.

On the second timeline baseball happens, has happened, will happen in a moment. Time does not elapse. I am, on this timeline, at some indistinct age, an age I have always been, and will always be. This is a public timeline, a reservoir into which we might all wade.

These two timelines are related. They occasionally snake and entwine, curl into one another, engage in dialogue and then fall apart, diverging until they are no longer proximate, a state in which they will exist until something forces their convergence. A moment that nudges them together.

*i. Roberto Alomar, American League Championship Series Game 4, October 11, 1992, Oakland-Alameda County Coliseum*

My parents occupy the couch and I am in an easy chair. We live in Ottawa's suburbs. The furniture matches. The carpeting is beige. My father has retired from the navy and now works in the private defense industry. The patio door is obscured by hanging aluminum blinds that sway and rattle against one another when stirred by the air pouring from the floor vent. The Blue Jays were down 6–1 but Roberto Alomar completes the comeback when he pokes Dennis Eckersley's sidearm-slung offering over the wall in right field. Eckersley is angry.

What do each of us carry that will one day steer our fate? We can't now know. Alomar is jubilant. He raises his arms over his head. I am sixteen years old, skinny, with a face hammered by cystic acne. I have read Hemingway and Homer, but have not yet read Alice Munro, nor Roger Angell. I raise my arms over my head. I am jubilant.

*ii. Joe Carter, World Series Game 6, October 23, 1993, SkyDome*

I have a girlfriend. She and I are with friends in the basement of a house in Blackburn Hamlet, the same subdivision where my parents lived when I was born. We're deep in the weeds of teenage self-seriousness—J. G. Ballard novels and writing our own poetry and lying on our backs in the dark listening to Leonard Cohen—but we're still watching the game. This is not something these friends would usually be doing, but among the vestiges of my childhood I cannot relinquish, baseball is the most tenacious. I will never successfully quit it. Besides, everyone in Canada is watching this game. No one is losing any teen-angst cred over it. When Joe Carter comes up with Paul Molitor on first and Rickey Henderson on second, I tell my friends that Carter will hit a home run. This doesn't represent any special insight on my part, just a wishful guess, the words of a boy from the mouth of a young man. Alfredo Griffin is on deck. The count is 2–2. Carter reaches down for a Mitch Williams pitch—low and a little inside—and lifts it over the wall in left. I hug my girlfriend, our friends. Carter leaps like a child, jumps and skips down the first-base line, pinwheels his arms as he nears second. He touches 'em all and is smothered at home plate. Fireworks spark and drift down from the SkyDome's roof. I jump and whoop and my head brushes the low ceiling. Soon I will betray my girlfriend because I am young and stupid, but she will eventually forgive me, undeserving as I am. She will still be my dear friend twenty years after Joe Carter's home run, long after the Dome is renamed Rogers Centre.

*iii. José Bautista, American League Division Series Game 5, October 14, 2015, Rogers Centre*

Christie is in Northern Ontario and the children are up late. Game Five is happening, ninety minutes down the highway from our house, and I cannot pry my attention away from the game to officiate their bedtime rituals. They drift into and out of the family room. I tell them to brush their teeth, but they ignore me. I run upstairs during a commercial break to separate the boys, who are wrestling on the bathroom floor, and I squeeze a dollop of Thomas the Tank Engine toothpaste onto each of their brushes. Then I go back to the TV. My second book will be released in six months and I don't know it yet but it will contain an essay about this very baseball game, and the things happening in it, and which are about to happen. I give up on getting the kids to bed. I'm too distracted by everything playing out on the field. This characterizes my parenting style: haphazard, inconsistent. This is the strangest, most thrilling baseball game I have ever seen, and I'm lit up just as I'd be if I were watching it as a kid. There is other evidence to suggest my immaturity too: I have been unkind, let friendships wither, hermited myself inside a life defined by my family and writing. I have wavered and doubted and let fear guide my actions.

After several delays, the Blue Jays are batting in the bottom of the seventh and the Rangers have made a string of mistakes, allowing Toronto to load the bases and score a run. Bautista comes up with runners on the corners and consigns a Sam Dyson pitch to history, and then flips his bat in a manner that will prove cipher-like: it's defiant and triumphant and/or it's unsportsmanlike and evidence of the degradation of our society.

My children have come downstairs to watch with me, two in their pajamas, one in his underwear. Bedtime is forgotten. A friend who had offered me a ticket to the game, immediately behind the Blue Jays' dugout, messages me the next day: YOU COULD HAVE BEEN THERE. No, I couldn't, I reply.

*iv. Edwin Encarnación, American League Wild Card Game, October 4, 2016, Rogers Centre*

In the days leading up to the Wild Card Game we were in Toronto for a family celebration of my father-in-law's seventieth birthday, but we were also there for our children. It was important to us that the city do its work on them, prodding and picking apart the ideas of normalcy to which they'd been exposed. It was time for them to marvel at the diversity of life and experiences in such a place. We wanted to settle back and watch the very real expansion of their boundaries. I spent an afternoon with Adelaide, who was then ten, and my four-year-old niece, taking the subway here and there, rocketing along beneath the city, emerging in places that were foreign to them, then ducking again into the tunnels. Adelaide was approaching the time when it's appropriate to entertain inappropriate questions. I wanted her curiosity to lead her to things that would startle and thrill her.

Christie and I have fed our kids a selection of natural wonders—mountains, lakes, oceans, rivers, fjords, animals—but have perhaps skimped on the human-made variety. So, on this trip we showed them mummies and Persian rugs and marble busts and suits of armour at the Royal Ontario Museum, took them through the alleys of Kensington Market, walked Queen Street West and Yonge Street. The Blue Jays won on Saturday night, and then again on Sunday afternoon, securing their spot in the Wild Card Game; we watched this on the TV in our Airbnb. We visited the CN Tower and dizzied ourselves by staring down through the glass floor, gazed across Lake Ontario at the point where the cloud cover cracked and was infiltrated by the sun. On the west side of the observation deck, from high above, we saw the Rogers Centre, closed, inert, waiting. A characterless hulk, perfectly still from our vantage, and yet for me buzzing with something latent, as all ballparks are. From the ground the building is ugly, I said to my daughter, but it's still one of my favourite places in the world—a charmless block of poured concrete with a white plastic bubble on top, the place where Carter and Bautista excited us and defined themselves.

Back home in Peterborough, as TV coverage of the Wild Card Game begins, I have no plan to get my children to bed on time. I make popcorn. Adelaide makes signs: GO JAYS GO, and WE'RE COUNTING ON YOU TO WIN THIS. Christie's in Northern Ontario again—she frequently is this time of year—but will be home in time to see the end of this game. Her plane lands at Toronto Island, within view of the dome, when the score is still 1–0. It's 2–2 after five innings, as she drives home from Toronto. Eventually I put the kids to bed, then return to the TV. It's still 2–2 in the ninth inning, in the tenth.

I'm not there—the same friend had offered me a ticket to the game, and again I declined. I'm fighting fatigue in the eleventh but there are runners on the corners and all Edwin Encarnación needs to do is hit a decent fly ball. Ubaldo Jiminez is pitching—and the O's regular closer, Zach Britton, saver of 47 games in the regular season, is not—and his first pitch to Encarnación meets wood and then rises up through the electric air and lands in the second deck. Encarnación stands with his arms above his head and drops his bat. I stand with my arms above my head. "Oh my God," I say. "Oh my God."

"Did they do it?" asks Christie, who is upstairs unpacking. "Oh my God," I say again. The stadium erupts in jubilation and disbelief. The TV broadcast will end with that buzz still apparent, the emotional currency of that place like a contact high transmitted via satellite to us at home. It's unlikely that a team's fans should ever know even one of these moments, but Jays fans have counted four. In the morning I will show the children the replay of Encarnación's home run over breakfast. I will watch it myself a dozen more times.

Events on these timelines occur in order, spaced out by intervals of time, but also concurrent, mutually haunting one another. Their relationship is one of proxy and distance, events that feel both intimate and alien, removed. The first is real only to me. I alone know of all its details: my kids' food preferences, where I left my keys, my state of mind. I share the second timeline with countless strangers. In some ways I am a fiction, an imprecise construct, but the baseball moments are indisputably real. They exist in the eyes of millions of people. They are recorded in box scores, game wraps, newspaper accounts. They are *official*.

De-centring—the gradual diminishment of ego—is a messy process, characterized by fits and starts, but one worth pursuing. That's what's being broadly described by the personal timeline. In the public timeline, pageantry and community entwine, and magic is glimpsed. It's the magnetic pull of aesthetic and emotional grandiosity which bends the personal, domestic timeline always eventually back toward the public one, where we celebrate baseball together. The two timelines are coupled by engagement—how I, in my private life, consume and interact with that larger public sphere, and in so doing incorporate it into my own private life. It becomes mine as it becomes yours.

The public is cleaner and more easily understood, even for all the mystery which engulfs it, because it unfolds in a linear fashion. Seasons follow seasons. Players age and retire. It suggests the probability inherent in the improbable, and so offers hope to the cloistered and practical personal timeline. The public timeline says that amazing things are possible. The personal timeline requires this information, bereft as it often is of such proof. *Keep going*, says the public timeline, and I, in the heave and tangle of the personal, resolve to do just that.

## DON'T STOP TO COUNT THE YEARS
(For Bones)

We lost John Prine in April of 2020, one point of light in the unimaginably vast universe of stars snuffed out by Covid-19. Maybe the best songwriter America ever had died in the pandemic, leaving us with an embarrassment of smart, funny, sad, and beautiful songs, plus a million people or so who'd learned to play guitar because they'd heard about this mail-man from Chicago who made everyone who heard him tear up a bit.

I can't play guitar, but Christie's Irish-Catholic-by-way-of-PEI family is lousy with pickers. And whenever they get to-gether there are liable to be a half-dozen guitars, and maybe a fiddle too, and those of us who can't play join in with our voices. We all butcher the words of familiar songs from Merle Haggard to Leonard Cohen, Nancy Griffith to Emmylou Harris. From Edmonton to Cavendish, in kitchens and living rooms, at campfires, reunions, weddings, and funerals, the fact that we've gathered is excuse enough for one of these singalongs.

There's a reasonably good chance that one of Prine's tunes will get the family treatment "Sam Stone," sometimes, or maybe a verse or two and the chorus of "Your Flag Decal Won't Get You Into Heaven Anymore." I remember a windy fall day on Birch Island, in Sand Lake, Ontario, when Christie's uncle Bones played "Paradise" as the orange and gold leaves fell on all sides of us. The kids and I sang along; I used that song as a lullaby when they were little, so they knew the words. That and "Take Me Out to the Ballgame." Christie would put them to sleep singing Prine's "Angel of Montgomery" and Cohen's "Famous Blue Raincoat."

My heart flutters at something in those songs, and it's the same flutter that baseball sometimes gives me: a recognition of lineage, and time passing, and things being handed along. How our entertainments and distractions can take on the dignity of labour if invested with enough care and love.

We bought our first house in 2001, the same month the towers fell, and moved in at the beginning of November. I'd gone back to Carleton University to finish a degree in history. We broke the lease on a truly awful apartment in Sandy Hill, Ottawa, and put all our stuff in storage in Christie's parents' garage, and were living in their basement. I had a desk in the windowless furnace room where I completed my assignments and churned out all the pages I was turning in to the first writing class I'd ever done, Rick Taylor's fiction workshop. On the morning of 9/11 I was getting ready for class. Christie had taken the day off work to negotiate our first mortgage. Her brother called her and said, "Turn on the TV."

This was just a month after we'd seen Ichiro in person for the first time, in Seattle. By the time we backed a U-Haul into the gravel driveway of our own little prefab bungalow, all of that—baseball, apartment living, the carefreeness of a long summer road trip—seemed so ancient as to be imaginary. The world had changed in a day.

A night or two after we moved into the house in Oxford Mills, I stood in the darkened kitchen fighting with the tuning knob of the radio, trying to capture a stubborn signal from New York. I got it just long enough to hear Luis Gonzalez beat the Yankees in Game Seven with his bottom-of-the-ninth base hit. Within days rain began coming through the ceiling in the very spot I'd stood listening. Soon after that we were up on the roof, re-shingling our new home. The accumulation of sweat equity had begun.

Those were days in the forge; we were being shaped, and in turn shaping ourselves. We were house-poor and overwhelmed. I was in school, working part-time in a music store in downtown Ottawa, and writing short stories. Christie had graduated three years earlier and almost immediately started her career as a wildlife biologist with the Government of Ontario at a field office in Kemptville, about ten minutes from our new home.

In his 2002 sophomore campaign, Ichiro's numbers dipped, which is to say they resembled somewhat more closely those of a mortal. He hit "only" .321 and stole just over half the number of bases he had as a rookie. He was also intentionally walked more than any other hitter in the American League. He still garnered MVP votes, and his defense was once again deemed Gold Glove-worthy. In July he was voted to his second All-Star Game—held that year in Milwaukee, and featuring Commissioner Selig's controversial decision to declare a tie in the eleventh inning rather than have the contest go deeper into extras. Ichiro started in right, went 0 for 2, and was replaced by the Devil Rays' Randy Winn. Christie and I were travelling, but we watched all this unfold on large TVs at Don Cherry's Sports Grill in St. John's, Newfoundland.

Ordinarily I'd have been watching with my father at my parents' house in the far east end of Ottawa, about an hour's drive from Oxford Mills. We usually went there on Sundays for dinner and laundry facilities, and whenever there was a big game on. Our little bungalow had no cable, no satellite TV, only a thirty-foot-tall aerial pinned to the end of the house that captured the broadcast signals of four or five stations, none of which showed baseball, though from October to June we could, through the use of extra wire and a coat hanger or two, watch *Hockey Night in Canada* on CBC. I kept up with baseball on the internet, with live updates or choppily streamed radio broadcasts. Blue Jays games came in clearly over the AM, and on some summer nights, driving home from an evening shift or class, I could pick up stations broadcasting games from New York for an inning or two before they faded out.

That summer we became acquainted with the flora of our property: a big lilac bush and clumps of peonies that would get beaten down by heavy rains only to rouse themselves when the sun returned. Devilish knots of jimson weed. Tall grasses near the back of our property, thick with grasshoppers, and the tall cedar trees on either side of the house. The expansive lawn was weedy and sparse except for the spot over the septic tank out back, where it was thick and lush. We got to know the fauna too: deer visited the yard often, and turkeys. There were mice in the attic, and a skunk took up residence under our woodpile. On spring nights the frogs' chirping could be heard through shut windows. Carpenter ants ate the plywood floor of the shed. When the snow melted a woodpecker would use that big antenna to sharpen its beak, and the sound was like a machine gun. Coyotes called down the moon, sounding eerily close. Farmers' fields occupied most of the area, but there was a dense plot of forest directly opposite the house, across the gravel road. One morning Christie drove into work to discover a tranquilized bear in a trailer in the parking lot; the bear technicians told her they'd caught it a couple of hundred metres from our place.

On August 14, 2003, the power went out, and it stayed off for days. It became clear quickly that it wasn't a local phenomenon. We'd eventually learn that more than fifty million people were without electricity, in most of Ontario, New York, Ohio, and throughout the northeast. It was a Thursday, and I was just starting a shift at the HMV at Bayshore Shopping Centre, in Ottawa's west end. The other employees and I had to sit tight in a darkened mall for hours in case the power came back on, until we got the go-ahead to leave from our regional manager. Christie picked me up and we went to my parents' house, since our well pump was electric and we had no generator. On the West Coast there was no power interruption. The Mariners hosted the Blue Jays that night. Toronto won, and Ichiro went hitless with a walk, lowering his average three points to .339.

In 2004 Ichiro became one of the eternals. He spent all summer chasing down George Sisler's record for base hits in a season, finally tying and overcoming the eighty-four-year-old record on October 1. He added four more hits before the season ended two days later. He also won the batting crown (.372), made his fourth straight All-Star Game appearance, received MVP votes for a fourth consecutive season, and was awarded another Gold Glove.

Christie and I were married that September. The previous Christmas she had given me a Blue Jays ticket package of six games. I gave her an engagement ring. We'd never thought much about getting married, but as time wore on, and we became entrenched in mortgages and car payments, we thought what the hell. But we decided to do it ourselves, like we did just about everything. As with renovations and repairs, our reasoning was primarily financial. We rented a tent and had it erected on her parents' back lawn. We made the invitations, decorated, and Christie and her friends baked dozens of cupcakes. We did hire a caterer, which was the biggest expense in the budget. We went to the liquor store and filled the car with cases of booze. Made mix CDs in place of a DJ. The music for the ceremony was performed by a trio consisting of Christie's uncles Billy and Bones (guitar and vocals) and her aunt Kathy (fiddle and vocals). At our request they learned Sandy Denny's "By the Time It Gets Dark," and the Jayhawks' "All the Right Reasons." Seated in chairs in the grass—pickin' and grinnin', as Billy puts it— they played us down the aisle and back.

Christie's friend offered us a timeshare in western Massachusetts for our honeymoon, so as newlyweds we drove around the Berkshires listening to Sun Kil Moon while the Red Sox and Yankees crossed swords for the AL East title. They seemed to play each other exclusively that month. We were home again when the playoffs began and the Sox came back from the dead to stun New York. When Boston finished their sweep of the Cardinals for their first championship in eighty-six years, I was sitting on the back step drinking some kind of pricey whisky, almost certainly a gift from Dad, listening on a battery-operated radio. The stars were out and I could see my breath. Christie had been listening with me but had gone to bed sometime in the late innings. I probably had to work in the morning, but I didn't want to miss history. Remember, this was when the Red Sox were still loveable; in the years afterward their success became routine and so we all came to hate them. But in 2004 they were hard not to cheer for, like the 2016 Cubs. In retrospect those century-long droughts, whether the result of curses or legacies of incompetence, are part of what makes baseball wonderful. There should be more multi-generational losing streaks, not fewer. Now we really only have Cleveland left, and I won't be cajoled into rooting for Cleveland, at least not until they change their name.

The only year in his first decade in America in which Ichiro failed to garner a single MVP vote was 2005. He had a disappointing season, which for Ichiro looked like 206 hits, 33 stolen bases, and a .303 average. He also hit 15 home runs, a figure that would stand as his career best, and was both an All-Star and a Gold Glove winner again. That was the year we got a dog, a Blue Heeler we named Rebus, after the Ian Rankin character. Rebus's coat was mottled near his rump, with light brown and white patches on his neck, chest, and forelegs. Ears like Yoda. He could run like the wind and jump like a spring. He once shot up from a lying position and bit me in the chest when I accidentally stepped on his tail in the dark. That was before he messed up a ligament in his hind right leg while chasing a frisbee, but even that didn't slow him down much. He was a bundle of muscle and teeth and piss and speed, but then he'd lie down and show you his belly and let you rub it. The top of his snout was another spot he liked, and the base of his black ears, which were fuzzed like velvet. Rebus was batshit crazy, with a head full of bees, but I loved the hell out of him.

❧

I came to think of life as possessing a rhythm, a cycle that bent but didn't break. Summer was too brief. The leaves changed, the snow came. The snow melted, Ichiro returned. The woodpecker. The baseball season began, the peonies flowered, and the lilac burst into fragrant bloom. Dandelions and mosquitoes. The days lengthened. Ichiro collected base hits. The season ended, playoffs began. The Mariners went home. The leaves changed. Frost, and then snow.

We started growing vegetables, and bought a used lawn tractor to cut all that grass. Changed our own oil, learned to solder copper pipe. Opened the windows on warm nights and drank wine while listening to Uncle Tupelo.

In truth, we really weren't country people. We were well-intentioned suburban kids. I've never raised a rifle to my shoulder. Ours was just about the only house in the area without a pickup in the driveway, a snowmobile in the garage, and a gun locker inside. I worked in the city, our friends lived there. If you were to tally up the amount of money we spent on gas driving to friends' houses in Ottawa, pubs and restaurants in Ottawa, concerts in Ottawa, the figure would be appalling. We were, the locals knew, tourists, albeit enthusiastic ones, who intended to stay.

What we were doing out there, among the corn fields, serenaded by the ghostly calls of passing freight trains, was figuring out who we wanted to be. Part of this likely amounted to personal myth-making, but we leaned into practicality, frugality, resourcefulness. These things became ingrained, as constant as the progression of seasons.

-->>)(<<--

Adelaide was born at a hospital in Ottawa in July of 2006, on a hot Tuesday morning riven by thunderstorms. Ichiro had helped Japan beat Cuba in the first World Baseball Classic that spring. In April Christie and I had flown to Chicago for one last pre-parental weekend. The Brewers were rude guests of the Cubs at Wrigley, winning by 14.

The arrival of a child tends to throw off your equilibrium. Everything changes, not the least of which are your sleep patterns. There are whole swaths of time for which I have photos but only scattered memories. Years of no money, years of snow, years of mistakes, years of effort and love.

In 2007 Ichiro played exactly zero innings at his natural position of right field. How have I forgotten this? The M's needed a centre fielder. Mike Cameron was long gone, and brass had apparently given up on the dream of Willie Bloomquist turning into something he wasn't. Adam Jones was not yet ready. Seattle signed José Guillén and gave him right field, so Ichiro slid to centre. He wasn't out of place—his speed gave him the ability to cover all that ground—but that big arm of his was wasted in the middle. His true habitat was right.

In that year's All-Star Game in San Francisco Ichiro hit what remains the only inside-the-park homer in the history of the Midsummer Classic. He smacked a ball to right-centre that hit the wall and took a goofy bounce—Tim Carver called it a "screwy carom" on the Fox TV broadcast—that befuddled Ken Griffey Jr. (then with Cincinnati). The AL won 5–4 and Ichiro was named the game's MVP.

Adelaide was just shy of a year old then, and she'd already been to the Hall of Fame. I was working at a tech company, spinning my wheels. I'd leave that job within a few months to stay home with our firstborn, and I would end up teaching her Ichiro's name while Christie went back to work.

The games are long but the seasons short. In the slipstream of lived experience they crawl by and then recede at an alarming rate. This is acutely sensed when milestones are hit, as when your kid graduates from grade eight and prepares to enter high school. That can't be right, you think, because just yesterday I was packing a little bag of Goldfish crackers and her sippy cup and then taking her to the park by the river and piggybacking her over to the swings, and Ichiro was the only player she could identify on TV.

We had satellite TV by 2008, which made it easier to follow along as Ichiro led the league in hits (213) for the fifth time in eight seasons, batted .310, and kept his All-Star and Gold Glove streaks alive—eight years and counting for both. Adelaide and I threw a ball in our big backyard. Christie interviewed for a job in Peterborough, where her government ministry had a large office. Christie's always been a perfectionist, and her own worst critic. When she came home from the interview and told me she'd tanked it, I suggested we'd better start getting the house ready to sell.

She got the job, of course. The house—which we cleaned, painted, redecorated, and fixed up in the space of about six weeks—sold quickly. In Peterborough we bought a house that looks shockingly like the one she'd grown up in. The house is about a year younger than I am, and is in sight of the public school Adelaide and her future brothers would attend. We weren't in the country anymore. Rebus, used to open space and trails to run unleashed, had some trouble adjusting.

The rhythms were the same, though. Summer was too brief. The leaves changed, the snow came. The snow melted, Ichiro returned. No woodpecker, but grackles. The baseball season began, the apple tree flowered, the privet hedge burst into fragrant bloom. Dandelions and mosquitoes. The days lengthened. Ichiro collected base hits. The season ended, playoffs began. The Mariners went home. The leaves changed. Frost, and then snow.

The boys were born in late winter, 2010, six weeks prematurely. Adelaide was excited, and also jealous. Two hundred and fourteen base hits for Ichiro, another All-Star nod, MVP votes, and a Gold Glove. A month in the hospital for Cormac and Theo, overcoming jaundice, learning to breathe on their own, to nurse, to keep food down. I could hold one of our sons in each hand. I would walk to the hospital, blocks from our house, to feed them through NG tubes several times a day, sometimes with Christie, sometimes without. They came home a couple of weeks before their due date. We were all together that summer, Christie on maternity leave, Adelaide suddenly having to share our attention, the boys taking turns keeping us awake. Tummy time on a blanket in the shade of the apple tree, the Blue Jays on the radio. I upgraded to the full MLB.TV package, so on weeknights I could catch part of the Jays game, and then later watch the Mariners. No full games, though—twin infants wouldn't allow for that much uninterrupted TV.

In 2011—the boys on solid food, Adelaide in kindergarten—Ichiro surpassed Edgar Martínez as the Mariners' all-time hit leader, but failed to hit .300 or collect 200 hits for the first time. In '12, with Seattle in the midst of a seemingly interminable rebuild, Ichiro asked to be traded in order, he said, to free up his roster spot for a younger player. He became, unthinkably, a Yankee. Adelaide was a Girl Guide. Cormac and Theo sometimes slept through the night.

In New York Ichiro wore the wrong number, switching from 51 to 31 in deference to Bernie Williams, who'd retired in 2006, and for whom the Bombers would retire number 51 in 2015.

In 2013 Ichiro was still in pinstripes, seeing action in 150 games for the Yanks, wherever they needed him—all three outfield spots, DH, pinch-hitting or -running. Rebus lost weight that summer, stopped eating, and had trouble walking. His spark grew dimmer. I rubbed his ears as he died in a veterinarian's office. Once he was gone I removed his leather collar, rolled it up, and took it home.

→→⟨⟨←

It wasn't until Ichiro was in a new phase of his career, first with the Yankees and then with Miami, as a role player, or an injury replacement, that I understood his appeal to me wasn't just his otherworldly accomplishments, that it actually had as much to do with John Prine as it did Ty Cobb.

Both baseball and roots music are presumed to possess an essential conservatism. Baseball's vaunted pastorality, to which I have indeed in a very small way contributed, is chained to its fear of change, its reluctance to follow other organizations like the NBA in championing social causes, and the overwhelming whiteness of its boardrooms, clubhouses, and fanbase. Likewise, you don't need me to tell you that country music isn't generally considered the most progressive or diverse of musical genres.

Ichiro and Prine ran counter to the apparent folksiness of their respective milieus. In Ichiro, baseball's cow-pasture creation myth was countered with cosmopolitanism, internationalism, and idiosyncrasy. He had great respect for those who'd played the game before him, but he didn't have to look, act, speak, or play exactly like them in order to exist in the same continuum. Prine was schooled in the folk tradition, as well as the Acuff-Rose songbook, and knew the work of everybody who ever played the Opry, but he was anti-war and pro-marijuana. He wielded tradition in the interest of a sweet, nonjudgmental liberal humanism. He looked people in the eye and he loved them, no matter their affiliations, and then he wrote devastating songs about them.

So much of what they each represented spoke to me during those meaty years of my life. With Ichiro it's tempting to think that his place in my pantheon was solidified by the simple fact that his arrival coincided with the onset of my adult responsibilities. But it's not merely when, or how long. It's not even his numbers or superheroic acts. Rather, he spent almost two decades demonstrating the value of discipline, the slow, dogged accumulation of skill and experience, and the dignity of an individual devoted to his craft. During the first ten years of his MLB career, when he was tearing up the American League, I was coming to understand that everything I valued required sustained, daily, honest effort. "Nothing worth doing ever came easy," Christie and I would say when we were hammering roofing nails, or installing new windows, or walking in circles in a dark room, bobbing up and down and trying to get a baby or two to fall asleep.

Ichiro was always there. It's true that a lot of players always seem to be there, playing baseball in the background, but longevity means so much more when backed with the extreme rigour that Ichiro applied his craft. Because you don't just show up and do what Ichiro did. You don't hit .372 with 262 base hits, or get over 200 hits a year for a decade, just by showing up. And that was what I wished to ingest and to, eventually, embody.

Over the course of his career—just his career in America, mind you, effectively his second act—we bought a house, got married, had children, moved to a new town, advanced in our careers. I published books. Our kids grew up. Ichiro was constant, and constantly amazing. And in his steady comportment I saw character.

I don't mean his lack of demonstration. I'm not interested in the idea of a "right way" to play. I don't want to hear that Mantle didn't showboat his homers. More often than not, that's just a coded swipe at younger non-white players. I'm on record as naming José Bautista's bat flip as one of the most exciting moments in Blue Jays history. I love Juan Soto's batter's box calisthenics. But Ichiro's quietness was distinct from the Gehrig-like stoicism that many associate with the integrity of the game. Ichiro's stillness arose from being in tune with minute vibrations, directly connected to the game's hidden rhythms. He was divining the essence of baseball, and that required concentration. He was mulishly stubborn, devoutly prepared, and fiendishly dedicated to playing the game the way he saw fit. His opacity was the by-product; the point was always his effort, and the sum was the excellence born of quiet investment and routine work.

I'm an overthinker. Always have been. I can't watch baseball for long without wondering how it fits into my life, and why it means so much to me. With Ichiro there were as many questions as answers, but what was evident was that he was living baseball, that for him it was a *way*.

And what was I looking for, throughout those years, if not a code, a system, a method of knowing the world? In Ichiro I found it—daily effort, slow accretion, quiet attention. Nothing worth doing ever came easy. Ichiro modelled that, putting together a career measured in decades, not games, in thousands, not ones. Some songs you hear once and forget, others you sing for the rest of your life.

# DOOLEY WOMACK

Horace Guy Womack was employed by four different Major League teams across five seasons, a serviceable bullpen righty who lost as many games as he won, though he managed to keep his lifetime ERA a shade below three. There'd be no reason to know his name if he didn't have such a great one: he went by Dooley, for reasons that are less than clear at this remove.

Then there's the bit part he played in a pair of larger dramas. First, he was traded to Seattle along with minor-league hurler Roric Harrison in August 1969 for Jim Bouton, an event chronicled in Bouton's infamous tell-all book *Ball Four*. Harrison was still three years away from the bigs, but his presence was apparently a bit of tonic for Bouton, who wrote searingly, "I'd hate to think that... I was being traded even-up for Dooley Womack."

The other story unfolded in the largely empty stands and backrooms of Sick's Stadium, the small and rickety former home of the minor league Rainiers, who'd been liquidated when the American League decided that Seattle was a viable expansion market. In the tradition of civic chicanery and capitalist bamboozling that characterizes major professional sport, the Pilots' existence was contingent on the construction of a state-of-the-art stadium. When the money failed to pour in the way the team's owners hoped it would, the situation got sticky, the stadium failed to materialize, and the team went bankrupt. Following Dooley's—and the Pilots'—only season in Seattle, the team was sold to a used-car salesman named Bud Selig who moved them to Milwaukee before the 1970 season and renamed them the Brewers. When they departed Seattle they left behind a legal mess the American League would eventually settle by admitting the Mariners to their ranks. The Kingdome—the promised state-of-the-art stadium—was built, served its purpose, and has been demolished in the years since.

-->>><<<--

I read Bouton's book a long time ago and it's possible I'd have never given Dooley a second thought had I not found myself working for a tech company smack in the middle of the 2000s. It was my first desk job. Our open-concept offices were housed in a converted UPS garage. There was a ping-pong table. On Fridays in the summer, we were treated to barbecues with free beer on tap. We were given winter coats, sweaters, and T-shirts emblazoned with the company's logo. The cafeteria was staffed by an award-winning chef; you typed your employee number into a keypad and the price of that day's special (pan-seared scallops, pulled-pork sliders) was subtracted from your account, like a cool breeze blowing through your paycheque.

The owner was a maniac. The CEO hobnobbed with prominent conservative politicians. The pay was low and the burnout rate high. Young programmers (of which I was not one) were treated as a renewable resource. It was a terrible job.

But the desktop internet was fast, and my tasks were largely mindless. With all that time to graze the boundless rolling fields of information, I naturally found Dooley Womack on baseball-reference.com, where I frequently spent time. From there, I conducted a Google Image search, and up popped Dooley's clean-shaven, Gomer Pyle-ish face grinning beneath a very obviously airbrushed Seattle Pilots cap.

I'd been fascinated by the Pilots since I was thirteen and learned about their existence in a book of baseball trivia I'd bought at the Hall of Fame gift shop. My imagination was fired. A big league team that existed for only one year! Accordingly, the Pilots came to represent for me doomed enterprises and elegiac what-coulda-beens, which maybe tells you more about me than it does the Pilots.

Dooley was the face of all that, so he became my avatar.

The other thing I had time for while seated at my work station was fantasy baseball. My user name was Dooley_Womack. My team name was the Pilots. I was in a league with a few people from the office, including a programmer from Cuba who was a big Yankees fan. He recruited all his Cuban buddies and they'd take to the league boards to talk trash in Spanish.

I learned that I was not great at fantasy baseball. It didn't matter that the league had unlimited roster moves. It didn't matter if I was first on the waiver wire. It didn't matter how carefully I pored over stats and massaged my lineup. I just wasn't good. My digital Pilots were, like the real thing, basement dwellers.

I never enjoyed it. I learned that to succeed in fantasy sports is to profit from the expected, which runs counter to everything I love as a fan. I want to revel in the unexpected, not lose another weekly head-to-head with the guy from shipping because of it.

We also played in a corporate softball league, which was its own special blend of fuckery. The league was a microcosm of everything wrong with the contemporary workplace. Instead of a blind mix of Harry Rosen suits, business-casual Dockers, and dorm-room chic fleece, we were all decked out in flex-fit caps and button-up jerseys with heather grey torsos, red raglan sleeves, the corporate logo screen-printed over our hearts. There was rampant sexism and testosterone-addled competitiveness alongside a simple desire for intra-office camaraderie, an insidious executive-plebe social divide—ambitious tech careerists alongside those of us feigning enthusiasm for the sake of keeping our jobs—and plenty of cheating.

During games, and especially during their beery aftermath, we learned more about one another than we wanted to. We came to understand that those of us who spoke of our abilities the most often possessed the least; we identified who lusted after whom; we saw plainly who would do or say anything to gain advantage, be it corporate or sporting. We heard one another's favoured epithets. We watched our colleagues swing and miss, flail, and react poorly to failure. We noted how difficult it was for any of us to arrive at an honest appraisal of our capacities.

I hated every minute of it. My salary increased as my understanding of what I was supposed to be doing dwindled. Finally, though—*finally*—family called me home. Christie had given birth to our first child, a daughter, and taken a year of maternity leave. When she returned to work, I quit to become Adelaide's primary caregiver. I've never been back: not to a corporate desk job, and not to organized softball. I quit playing fantasy sports too.

⟶≫≪⟵

Part of what appeals to me about the Pilots, beyond the sweet tragedy of their short life, is their logo: a baseball inside a ship's wheel, flanked by a pair of golden wings. It's a lovely, albeit confusing, emblem, attempting as it does to speak both to Seattle's maritime history as well as to its aeronautical significance.

I like to think of Dooley Womack wearing it on his chest, decked out in the Pilots' cream home uniform, jogging to the mound from the bullpen at Sick's Stadium before a backdrop of empty seats, wondering how he'd gotten there, and how long he'd be made to suffer in that particular workplace.

As it happened, he was bound for Oakland, though his career was effectively over. He appeared twice for the A's in 1970, pitching a total of three innings. He held on in the minors for another year.

The logo's golden wings unwittingly presaged the Pilots' quick departure from the Pacific Northwest, to say nothing of the countless flights of home runs off their opponents' bats. But I wonder if Womack took some solace from those wings, as I do, and their suggestion of the comfort located in knowing that these matters will yet prove fleeting.

# CONVERGENCES

Yordan Álvarez is depicted on the Topps 2020 Series One Variation #276 in glorious landscape orientation, like a widescreen Panavision vista of mesas and buttes, the fever dream of John Ford ardently lusting after a sunset into which he might send his hero trotting. Álvarez possesses plenty of swagger, but on this card he does not appear heroic. He looks defeated as he makes the long walk back to the dugout, a look of frustration on his face, or possibly anger, eyes cast into the middle distance, his mouth a thin, tight line. And this is not the frontier; it's a ballpark.

Álvarez made his major league debut for the Houston Astros on June 9, 2019, and this card was issued in February of 2020, which means the photograph was taken sometime during the latter half of his first season. Over his shoulder looms the unmistakable sight of Camden Yards' B&O Warehouse, so he's in Baltimore. Houston visited the Charm City only once that season, for a three-game set in August, so we can assume the shot was taken on one of those three dates.

Further, Álvarez isn't wearing the Astros' standard road greys, nor is he sporting the orange or navy alternate jerseys Houston has been known to wear. He is instead wearing a throwback uniform—a modern version of the getup the Astros donned from 1982 until 1993, the name Astros across the chest in an Arial-like sans-serif font, navy blue over a plain navy star. Above that, things get weird: thick racing stripes of navy-red-orange-gold-orange-red-navy drape the shoulders. This was the toned-down version of their 1970s tequila sunrise uniforms, which we can only guess made sense at the time, but now look like a parodic representation of what that decade felt like if you were tuned in, pharmacologically.

His batting helmet is navy, unlike the bright orange lids those '70s Houston teams wore—hunter blaze, we'd call them now, usually complemented by a full neck-to-toe camo ensemble, the cap designed to make you decidedly not ungulate in the eyes of fellow sportspeople lurking in the bush with trigger fingers made itchy by hours of inaction.

An odd thing about those '82–'93 Astros uniforms is that there was no true road version. At home they wore white, and on the road they sported the very same uniform in cream. But Yordan Álvarez, it appears to my eyes, is wearing white on the card. Of all the orthodoxies I hold dear to my heart, this is among the strictest: a ballclub should wear white at home and grey—or in very select cases, powder blue—on the road. Ever was it thus, ever thus should it be.

Check the actual home team's promotional schedule for the 2019 season and you'll find that on August 9 the O's were celebrating the 1989 "Why Not?!" Orioles, a team of scrap and grit that came close to winning the AL East, heading into the season's final weekend needing a sweep of the Blue Jays to take the division. The Jays won two of three.

But the Frank Robinson-led Orioles had taken their fans on such a great ride that thirty years later, in the midst of a miserable 108 loss season, the 2019 O's dressed up in 1989 uniforms to mark that exciting run, and the Astros played along by wearing period-appropriate (if not geographically consistent) togs. Never mind that in 1989 the Astros were a National League club and so, short of a World Series matchup, would never be in Baltimore to play the Birds.

When commemorating what once was, we often get the details a little bit wrong.

--->>><<<---

I pulled Series One Variation #276 from a retail pack sometime back in March, and ever since the card has held me in wild fascination. The effect is oversized in relation to my regard for Álvarez; I'm basically indifferent to him. I've only ever given

Yordan Álvarez—an imposing, Aaron Judge-like presence in the middle of the Astros' order—a passing thought as an avatar of modern baseball. But the card is mesmeric, a small object around which gravity bends subtly but perceptibly.

This is what the best cards do, whether they're of our favourite players, or feature an odd quirk or error, or otherwise manage to imprint themselves in the folds of our soft brains and stick there. They carry a series of signals betraying disparate and competing energies, emitting a persistent, high-pitched buzzing.

This one buzzes with questions that zip like unruly voltages. Like: why that uniform? And given it's clear from his carriage that he has just struck out: is there still room for shame in a post-shame world?

Álvarez' slow, simmering post-K saunter is anything but exceptional; it's what he did in over 25 percent of his plate appearances in 2019. Historically speaking, that's remarkable, but in the narrow trough of these launch-angle days, it's par for the course: the average strikeout rate across baseball was 23 percent in 2019, an astonishing new historical high.

When tabulated, collated, filtered, and parsed, the numbers tell us that the Rob Deer approach of Three True Outcomes—i.e., homering, striking out, or walking, all representing a steadfast refusal to put the ball in play—wins ballgames. It's a style of baseball condoned by the cubicle-dwellers for whom the ones and zeroes of absolute efficiency trump aesthetic arguments, because the Datapoints Do Not Lie.

But here's the friction: despite what the numbers say, the human soul still harbours a strong vestigial dislike of failure, and the one-on-one nature of the hitter-pitcher dialectic makes the called third strike or the big-swing-and-a-miss look unmistakably like failure. The strikeout elicits micro-scale stirrings of shame. It can't be helped. Nobody likes to whiff, and Álvarez is no exception, though his debut campaign would suggest an attempt at immersion therapy.

Álvarez' photo on Series One Variation #276 reflects that unavoidable distaste. His face is captured in a candid moment of naked emotion, a sliver of time tucked beneath the game's joints and surfaces. He should no longer be the focus of attention, having ceded it to Carlos Correa, who followed him in the lineup. But the camera found him, and the result is a wonderful photo, with echoes of the great John Dominis shot of Mantle dejectedly throwing his batting helmet while retreating to the Yankee Stadium dugout in 1965.

Anyway, what Álvarez did in 2019 when not striking out was noteworthy: .313, 27 HR, 78 RBIs in 369 plate appearances after his early June call-up, and a unanimous selection as 2019 American League Rookie of the Year. That trophy was supposed to belong to Toronto's Vladimir Guerrero Jr., but Vladito turned in a performance that evinced mortal fallibility instead of the demigod we'd been promised, while Álvarez came in and raked. The choice was clear.

—»»×«««—

The game log for August 9 informs us that Álvarez singled in the top of the first to score Alex Bregman from second; in the top of the third, Álvarez struck out swinging on Baltimore starter Dylan Bundy's 1–2 offering; he struck out swinging again in the top of the sixth, once more Bundy's victim, on an 0–2 pitch; in the eighth, Álvarez hit a fly ball off reliever Paul Fry to left that was caught by Anthony Santander for the second out. That was Álvarez's night: 1-for-4 with a single, an RBI, and two strikeouts. The Astros won 3–2.

The photo in question must be from the third-inning K, because the sky behind Álvarez's head, over the great brick warehouse, is purplish, heavy-seeming, but not yet dark. At that time of year, in that part of the world, the sun sets shortly after 8:00 p.m., and first pitch that night was 7:17 p.m. By the time Álvarez struck out for the second time, night had fallen.

The next night the Astros walloped Baltimore 23–2, with Álvarez homering three times, including a grand slam, for a total of seven RBIs. But the Yordan Álvarez of Friday night's third-inning strikeout is of greater interest to me. He stands at the nexus of innumerable convergences: strains of information, history, prognosis and apology, wayward currents pinched to a single point in space. He's an individual upright but unguarded, caught in 1/100th of a second and preserved against a familiar background, that great brick facade vivid but blurred, which suggests that he is stalked by uncertainties. The thick, hazy air of a dog day's evening makes time's immateriality evident. Much has come unmoored.

There's a lot to be said about the Houston Astros circa 2017–19, both about the accusations preserved in official accounts and related disciplinary reports, and the many deeds suspected but unproven. Nobody's linked Yordan Álvarez' great rookie season to electronically abetted sign stealing, but the suspicion may follow him anyway, as it will everyone connected to that team during those years. Stains spread.

It's also possible that you don't think what Houston is purported to have done constitutes anything but the logical progression of the time-honoured baseball tradition of action and reaction—the interception of the enemy's cryptographic messages to gain competitive advantage, updated for the twenty-first century yet still spiritually linked to practices dating to the nineteenth. But it feels safe to assert that the Astros are emblematic of shifting values and practices that make modern baseball feel morally ambiguous. For a hundred years there was, at least, a Right Way to do things, and a Wrong Way. The in-game definition of virtue was skewed and problematic, but it was at least a definition. Now a cold integer logic means fewer stolen bases and fewer manager ejections, and it makes homers feel cheaper by virtue of oversupply. We've allowed the old gods to die and replaced them with Win Probability. You might understand why these things have happened, and yet still long for the old structure the way an atheist envies the adherent's certainty.

Yordan Álvarez is connected to all this, but not implicated. He plays baseball the way he's been taught and trained to play it, and he does it well, and the rewards are plain. Series One Variation #276 is just a baseball card. But I look at it in something like the narcotized daze of phone hypnosis, this smooth and glossy cardboard rectangle, hints of the mystery with which all such mementos are imbued, images of figures in collision with history, men bound by contracts, time working its silent will. The tracers are barely visible but strangely evident, those countless converging forces, smell of popcorn and beer, close summer nights full of love and torpor, and all our accidental associations.

# MADE TO BE BROKEN

Baseball, more than other sports, is preoccupied with records. They are the primary language by which the contemporary game communicates with its past version, or versions. Records are yardstick as well as legend, lingua franca and litmus. Use them to support or refute. Use them to argue or agree. The apocryphal book that contains baseball's records is large, unwieldy, and overfull. You can find anything you might be looking for in there and use your findings to bolster just about any bias you might harbour about this baffling, flawed, perfect, beautiful game.

In any discussion of baseball records, one fault demands mention. Every benchmark established before Jackie Robinson's debut in 1947 is at best dubious, stained because the American and National Leagues did not fully represent the populations of those constituencies their names invoked. Generations of Black and Latin American ballplayers—some whose names we know, like Josh Gibson and, for most of his best years, Satchel Paige, as well as many we don't—endured America's segregationist policies as enforced by baseball's power structure, and so their numbers were not fairly weighed against those of their white counterparts. In fact, we should mark with an asterisk all records made before midseason 1959 when the Red Sox, who'd shamefully been the last team to integrate, sent Pumpsie Green in to pinch run for Vic Wertz.

In many cases, major-league records of simple accumulation, like strikeouts or RBIs, were tallied against inferior competition, as many of the better or even best players were not allowed to compete on the game's largest stage, but were confined to the Negro Leagues, Latin American circuits, or independent travelling teams, their records and achievements recorded in scattered annals. Only recently have researchers begun to amass a complete picture of these players' efforts.

The composite makes clear that, in baseball terms the performances we did not see, the numbers amassed in games unsanctioned by the national press represent an enormous loss. In human terms the loss is even more incalculable.

But those pre-integration performances are still official by MLB standards, and records that were established then still need to be toppled the old-fashioned way, by bettering them.

Records, then, sort neatly into two categories: some stand, most fall. The records in the first category—those that we feel some security in claiming will never be bettered—are few in number, but let's hazard some guesses: Cobb's batting titles—12 overall, and 9 in a row; DiMaggio's 56 consecutive games with a hit; Cal Ripken's 2,632 straight games played; and almost certainly any pitching record notable for the duration, longevity, or workload required to set it, like Ed Walsh's modern era mark of 464 innings pitched for the 1908 White Sox. Records for basestealing likewise seem safe for the time being, as the running game is all but extinct, so Rickey Henderson's career stolen base total of 1,406 is likely ironclad.

Of course, records *do* move from one bucket to the other, because we really don't know how the game will evolve. Just when we begin to speak with certainty about an untouchable mark, someone rises to threaten it. Our vision is imperfect.

In 1920, George Sisler established a high-water mark for base hits in a season. The first baseman played all 154 games for the St. Louis Browns that year, collected 257 hits (including 49 doubles and 18 triples), stole 42 bases, knocked in 122, all while batting .407. That the lowly Brownies managed only a fourth-place finish speaks to the quality of the rest of the roster. After a "down" year in '21 (216 hits, .371 average, 35 stolen bases) he outdid himself in 1922, leading the league with an absurd .420 average but totalling a *mere* 246 hits, still good for best in the American League.

For better than eight decades, it was unthinkable that anyone would improve upon Sisler's 257 hits in a season. It ranked among the untouchable records. That is, until Ichiro went ahead and bettered it in 2004.

That Sisler's name now fails to elicit the recognition of a Cobb or a Hornsby or a Wagner is something of a head-scratcher. He was a protégé of Branch Rickey, the man who eventually signed Jackie Robinson to the Brooklyn Dodgers, and who changed the way major-league ball was structured by reorganizing the relationship between big-league teams (specifically the Cardinals, where he landed after the Browns) and the minors, and building the first true farm system. Sisler followed Rickey, his coach at the University of Michigan, to the Browns, where the younger man was seen as a pitcher as well as a first baseman. By 1916 he was a full-time first sacker and flexing his muscles as a serious hitter. Not, mind you, as a home run hitter—his career high of 19, established in that dizzying season of 1920, hardly qualifies him as a slugger. Ruth was inventing that role contemporaneously to Sisler's successes, just as Sisler was mastering the game as played by Cobb and other stars of the Deadball Era.

As a measure of his renown, it's worth noting that in 1925 it was Sisler—not Ruth, not Cobb, not Walter Johnson—who was the first ballplayer to appear on the cover of *Time* magazine, which had begun publishing in 1923.

And he might have ascended to even greater heights had he not lost the entire 1923 season to complications from a severe sinus infection that left him with double vision. He returned in 1924 and was an effective hitter and the same sure fielder he'd been, but he never again threatened .400. He did crack 200 hits three more times. His playing days lasted until 1930, the last three of which he spent with Boston's National League club (with a brief stop in Washington). By the time he retired, the game had been wholly made over in the image of his contemporary, Ruth. In 1915, Sisler's first season in the bigs (and the Babe's second), Gavvy Cravath of the Phillies led the majors with 24 home runs and paced the National

League with 89 runs scored. In Sisler's last campaign, fifteen years later, the Cubs' Hack Wilson was tops with 56 homers, and the Phils' Chuck Klein had scored 158 times to lead all of baseball in that category.

By the twilight of his playing days Sisler was a holdout, a throwback to a turn-of-century style of play that would eventually fall out of favour, a game played with scuffed, beaten, muddy balls, in enormous ballparks, in which the real fun began when the ball was put in play.

Sisler held onto his record for hits in a season for better than eight decades; it was unbeatable, until it wasn't. In 2004, Ichiro collected his 258th knock late in the season with members of Sisler's family in attendance in Seattle. Ichiro finished the season with 262 hits on the year. He had 924 hits over the first four seasons of his Major League career, a total no one had ever achieved in a four-year span.

In addition to the record, Ichiro won the batting title with a .372 average, but finished seventh in American League MVP voting. Vlad Guerrero of the Angels took home the trophy. Guerrero had 39 homers. Ichiro had 8.

Life always speeds up. Subtlety and nuance are ever fighting a rearguard action. By 2004 the acceleration had reached the point of infinite feedback, the high squealing sound of information devouring itself and outputting nonsense. A game like Ichiro's, built on guile, patience, and opportunity, was only ever going to be tolerated, not celebrated in the way that 70 home runs was celebrated, or in the way that a ball launched 450 feet is celebrated. This is because baseball now resembles baseball only by virtue of its irreducible *baseballness*, the presence of bats and balls and caps and pinstripes.

Ichiro arrived an outsider, which gave him the freedom to eschew the status quo and parlay his natural gifts to resurrect a style of play that Babe Ruth helped bury, a game that exploited the seams of the modern style, a game more interested in every blade of grass on the field than the wall that demarcated its boundary.

In reaching back to Sisler's game, and besting Sisler's record, Ichiro entered into a dialogue with that lost era of baseball, connecting it with this harried and muscle-infused culture of immediacy. Such conversations with the dead remain vital. We're now barely on speaking terms with the game as it was played in Sisler's time. As the pace of change increases, we're in danger of losing the language altogether.

But this, really, is why we keep records: to preserve the dialect, and to compare the incomparable. We have no sword in the stone, no heroic tests, save these numbers. They allow us to place individuals separated by a decade or a century alongside one another and gauge their relative accomplishments. It's an imperfect system. The game changes. But baseball's records—surpassed or insurmountable—are the means of communication between the eras. If you're going to play catch with ghosts, you need something to toss back and forth.

# I SHALL NOT PASS THIS WAY AGAIN

After Labour Day, we watch summer recede in the rearview with alarming speed until it resolves into a single point, the way a slider is said to reveal itself to hitters with the appearance of a red dot. It might still be hot where you are, but the light has changed in ways that portend the end of the hot months' bright carelessness, and the onset of a long-shadowed twilight.

In late August I grabbed the kids and our passports and drove three hours from Peterborough to Buffalo, where the AAA Bisons—the Blue Jays' top farm club—were ending their season with abundant giveaways, one-dollar popcorn, and fireworks. We crossed the border and joined sixteen thousand others in the stands at what was then called Coca-Cola Field (it was renamed Sahlen Field in 2019), and we weren't in our seats long when Vladimir Guerrero Jr. poked one over the wall in left-centre. We filled ourselves with carbonated drinks and fried bologna sandwiches, and a smoky, big full moon floated over the ballpark.

The Bisons eventually fell to Pawtucket, but that didn't seem all that noteworthy as the shells exploded above our heads in red and green and blue and white splashes, and my kids whooped and screamed and laughed. After the last of the smoke blotting the moon drifted over Swan Street, we headed for the gate in no particular hurry to get anywhere, though we were suddenly on the wrong end of a three-hour drive. Leaving, we all intuited, meant saying goodbye to what had been a very good summer, though it was then not yet September.

The whole evening had been joyful, but its edges were infused with a warm melancholy, tinged with the soft grief we share in the dimming of our sweet and trivial warm-weather entertainments. There's also a feeling particular to minor league ballparks at that time of year, a loneliness and a reflexive kick against the thought of a winter spent without baseball.

I understand that summer doesn't actually end on Labour Day, but that's when the season begins to strain at its seams, to betray its porousness, the shorter days and the chillier nights admitting a vulnerability. The kids are back in school, but they're wearing shorts, though the ease of summer is suddenly gone, its wide openness, its possibility for adventure and aimlessness.

On the drive home from Buffalo, after we'd crossed back over the border and the highway unclogged, all three of my children fell asleep, and I lapsed into a feeling I'd had only the week before, as we'd driven through wet weather on our way home from vacation in the Catskills. Near the Finger Lakes we'd passed gorges and modest valleys where mist had collected, opaque and soft-edged, like milk in a bowl. It was beautiful. But what was I to do with that? I wanted to stop and take photos, though I knew they would fail to capture what I saw. I knew too that I might never see those valleys again, those gorges, that particular heavy mist. The urge to document bumped against the desire to experience. I didn't stop to pull out my camera, deciding instead to look hard, to imprint the images to memory. To absorb the sights as moments in which I resided, rather than opportunities I was missing. And yet I found myself dipping toward grief for something that was not quite gone, but that would soon be carried by its own momentum to a place I could no longer reach.

# THE SENSE OF AN ENDING

In Hollywood's version of *The Natural*, Roy Hobbs's final on-field act is a glory-soaked one. In Bernard Malamud's novel, though, Hobbs bows out in shame. It's a perfect illustration of the difference between pop culture and literature, a painful novelistic hewing to the difficult facts of life versus the Hollywood movie's wishful apotheosis. It's illustrative too of a certain basic truth: the ending we want is seldom the ending we get.

The example of Ken Griffey Jr. is an instructive one. In 2008, after eight-plus seasons in Cincinnati, Junior bounced from the Reds to the White Sox, where he failed to prove his continued relevance at age thirty-eight. Then came what seemed a fitting denouement: the one-year deal to return to Seattle for a last hurrah. It was a respectable campaign for Griffey: 19 home runs, 57 RBIs. So he signed for another year, but in 2010, at age forty, Junior's skills seemed to drop precipitously. It was difficult to watch: he was a shadow of his old self, even if that younger version did occasionally pop up. Manager Don Wakamatsu drastically reduced the aging star's playing time; Junior took up residence on the bench or, as one anecdote had it, took to napping in the clubhouse. By early June, with the Mariners in last place, Junior was hitting .184 and could ignore the signs no longer. He left Seattle in the middle of the night, driving home to Florida. He sent notice of his retirement from the road.

Junior finished his career with 630 home runs, and was deservedly enshrined in Cooperstown by near-unanimous consensus. As with a lot of the all-time greats, though, the end was messier than the beginning, and less tidy than it might have been. The signs were there for all to see but the man himself, until it was too late for a dignified send-off. That's all obscured now by the mutual love between Griffey, the Mariners, his fans, and the people of Seattle—his number has been retired, his statue stands outside the gates of T-Mobile Park (as Safeco Field came to be known in 2019). But it's tempting to wonder how much cleaner it all could have been had The Kid chosen to bow out after his decent 2009 campaign.

Which brings me, uneasily, to Ichiro.

➵➵⊷⊷

In Seattle, Ichiro witnessed the twilight and conclusion of Edgar Martínez' brilliant Hall of Fame career. Edgar bowed out in 2004, announcing in August that it would be his final season. That year was marred by injury—Martínez' legs and back were deteriorating, as were his eyes. In his second-to-last season, at age forty, he was an All-Star and a Silver Slugger winner. A few injuries nagged, but Edgar was still a very effective big-league ballplayer. Once it became clear to him that his body would not allow him to perform at the level to which he was accustomed, Martínez made what I can only assume is the hardest decision a ballplayer will make.

I never wanted to watch Ichiro's greatness decline into ruin. If entropy is universal, clearly it happens at differing rates. He had made known his desire to play long past most players' best before dates, which, if he got his way, would mean he'd still be slapping base hits when Adelaide was ready to start university. It was tempting, during the later years of his career, to seize upon moments of athletic grace—his wall-climbing catch of a deep fly ball to left by Cleveland's José Ramirez in the second game of the 2018 season, for instance—in order to fuel the belief that he'd have his way. But that required ignoring certain other evidence, such as the incremental but noticeable drop in bat- and footspeed.

Ichiro was not, to be precise about things, a part of the Mariners' plans in 2018. Injuries to several players in spring training made him a temporary solution, but once everyone healed he was, realistically (or perhaps even charitably), the fifth-best outfielder in the organization. It pains me more than you might imagine to state it, but at forty-four years of age Ichiro was not the ball-vacuuming fielder he had been, and he was being thrown out on the sort of ground balls he once routinely beat out for base hits. Ichiro was no longer the sort of player apt to propel his team to additional victories. His presence was not compatible with the team's goal of winning baseball games.

Roster spots on a big-league club are finite—there were twenty-five in 2018—and they must be spent wisely. In a move apparently designed to accommodate Ichiro and his accumulated status, Guillermo Heredia, clearly the better option to fill the fourth outfielder's slot, was sent down to the minors. Ichiro was used to fill odd spots, as a late-inning designated hitter or pinch runner, or infrequent left fielder. His numbers weren't good, though, and historically players of his vintage don't rebound all that dramatically.

There were bright spots: the day Heredia was sent down to AAA Tacoma, Ichiro started in right field—his old position—and had a fine afternoon; he went 2-for-3 with a pair of walks in a loss to Texas. Ichiro Suzuki wasn't an effective everyday player anymore, but it was not then clear if anyone had told that to Ichiro Suzuki yet.

I don't know who's ultimately responsible for these things. Who lets a future Hall of Famer know that his time is up? Is it up to the future Hall of Famer to know it himself?

Maybe there isn't another way. Maybe the fire that made a player like Ichiro as good as he was for so long is the same heat that prevents individuals from giving up the fight until they're forced to do so. It's important, in a game as dependent as baseball is on the Sisyphean repetition of small tasks over a long season, that every ballplayer believes he's one good game—a 3-for-4, a leaping catch against the wall—from rediscovering his groove. There comes a time, though, for even the greatest players, when that ceases to be true, when the past is at odds with the present, the two commingling less than comfortably until finally something must give.

⇢⇤⇤

For all its avowed fondness for the unexpected, for twist endings and spontaneous celebration, baseball loves its staged moments. In this way does it most effusively congratulate itself—banners unfurling, speeches rehearsed, fabric draped over statuary, a microphone placed on the pitcher's mound for the pre- or in-game ceremony. But sometimes we don't know with certainty that we're witnessing history, or its end. Sometimes we're not told, and it just happens, and only later is something confirmed, via press release, or word leaking out, a comment to a seasoned beat reporter, a player going off-script. And then we fans go back and review the moment, and, yup, that was it. That was history.

The effective end of Ichiro's career came on May 2, 2018, with one out in the bottom of the ninth inning of a Wednesday night game at home against the Oakland Athletics, with runners on first and second, the Mariners trailing 3–2. Imagine the sound inside Safeco Field had the assembled known the significance of the moment. But the news hadn't yet come. There was an inkling that Ichiro was nearing the end, but nothing had been officially proclaimed.

Ichiro struck out. The next hitter, Dee Gordon, singled to load the bases before Jean Segura grounded out to end the game.

There's no terrific shame in striking out, especially in the modern game. Ichiro did it over a thousand times in his major-league career. But you couldn't help but feel that the old Ichiro would have slapped a base hit in that situation, or laid down a perfect bunt. And imagine he had; a seeing-eye single to score a run, possibly two. What an ending that would have been, even if we hadn't known, in the moment, that it was the end.

If we are fortunate, we organize our lives to accommodate both love and constancy, though the latter is nearly impossible to find. Ichiro made it seem tantalizingly proximate. He was already twenty-seven years old when he debuted with the Mariners, and he played in nineteen seasons thereafter. He operated on a time scale different from most mortals. Still, time won't be denied forever.

What made the prospect of him continuing to play so alluring for me was not simply the pure aesthetic joy of watching him toil in a fashion so idiosyncratic and stylistically anomalous that it seemed he was playing a different game altogether, but that his familiar presence put me in touch with the person I was a long time ago, and a time from which I am otherwise exceptionally distant. Ichiro hit a ground-ball base hit off Blue Jays closer Billy Koch in the ninth inning of a game on August 9, 2001. Christie and I were sitting down the third-base line at Safeco, at about the midway point of the road trip that would take us from Ottawa, ON, to Victoria, BC, and back again, through the American Great Plains, transecting the Rockies, to the Pacific, and back across the Canadian Prairies. We were in our mid-twenties, childless, without even an apartment, the sum total of our material possessions stowed in her parents' garage, waiting for our next move. We had a two-person tent and a pair of sleeping bags in the trunk. We listened to cassettes as we drove, navigated with maps, and kept our minds busy with a stack of cards from an old copy of Trivial Pursuit. We saw *Rush Hour 2* in Fargo, North Dakota. We took photos using rolls of film.

Ichiro was already an All-Star, already well on his way to the 242 hits he would collect that year. He was already the player he was to be for all the seasons to follow, established in his routines, faithful to his ritualistic methods of preparation and concentration. In the ninth inning on that night in August he arched his back to both sides, crouched to the ground, then stood in the batter's box and held his right arm out toward the pitcher, the bat in his right hand perfectly still, perpendicular to the earth. He brought his left hand across his chest and gave a small tug to his right sleeve near the shoulder before swinging the bat around and back behind his left ear. He took a pitch, which the umpire called a ball, then repeated the above. The second pitch he lashed at and drove into shallow right field, advancing Stan Javier to second. The next hitter singled behind Ichiro, and then Edgar Martínez singled to score both Javier and Ichiro. The rally died thereafter when John Olerud grounded out, and the Mariners went down to the Blue Jays, one of just 46 losses they'd suffer that year.

That ponderous at-bat ritual—thousands and thousands of instances of it, before every swing, in each game, for nine seasons in the NPB, and nineteen campaigns split between the Mariners, Yankees, and Marlins—was as much a timing device as it was a philosophical expression, a willful slowing of time, a location of stillness in the action around him. That he did it so identically for so long, though the world continued to spin and howl, was enormously reassuring. This provided me a bridge, amid personal chaos and evolution, home owner-ship and marriage, the births of children, losses, errors, successes, projects failed and abandoned, hopes achieved, from the twenty-five-year-old me to the middle-aged version. And though so much appeared to have changed, Ichiro's continued presence, and the bankable sameness of that routine, suggested to me that some things can be constant.

But then an ending came, and it was every bit as inscrutable as Ichiro himself. He stepped aside, making room for younger and, indeed, more capable outfielders, and accepted the role of special advisor to the chairman, a position created specifically for Ichiro, apparently using a roll of Scotch tape and all the business jargon they could find. In substance the job looked exactly like his playing days, minus the playing; he travelled with the team, dressed in uniform, took batting and fielding practice, and when the game began he ducked into the clubhouse where he continued to stretch and exercise.

But the language was vague, and steered purposefully away from the use of the term "retirement." Ichiro had not filed those particular papers yet, which meant that he maintained the freedom to return to the game, should the opportunity arise.

I saw him again shortly thereafter, for what was the final time in person. I'd made plans to see the Mariners in Toronto with my friend, the poet Rob Winger, and we'd bought tickets at field level down the left-field line in the hopes that Ichiro would be playing. When the announcement of Ichiro's new non-playing role was made, just days before the game, our focus shifted: we had to see if he was actually there, taking batting practice, loping across the outfield shagging flies, making effortless behind-the-back catches.

We arrived before the gates opened, and we rushed inside the cavernous Rogers Centre. There, in right field, beneath the sun streaming down through the open roof, stood Ichiro, talking to teammates, laughing, joking, stretching, barely interrupting any of this to reach up and snag fly balls. He seemed lighter, less burdoned relaxed. After a while he sprinted into the dugout, where he began his familiar stretching routine. Then he strode out across the turf and into the batting cage, where he proceeded to spray balls all over the field, and some into the second deck. He stepped out to allow another player his pitches, and then moved back in, hitting more home runs, more sharp liners, balls hitting the fence on one hop, balls stung and lashed and pounded; an art form enacted not for an audience but for the pure aesthetic exercise of it, hitting for hitting's sake. For his own sake.

And so Ichiro—who'd once supposed that he would die when he was done playing baseball—had uncovered some strange kind of baseball afterlife. Or was it a purgatory? If the latter, it seemed unusually blissful, because he'd found a way to remain in touch with the person he used to be—in his team's uniform, sprinting across the turf, taking his cuts— while also wearing a smile that suggested to those of us watching that there might be life yet, after the demise of the things we believed gave us life, at least when we were young.

# JIM BEAM

I write this from a subterranean lair packed tight with books, CDs, LPs, cassettes, an old laptop or two, a pile of baseball memorabilia. Accrued relics. Things. This is where I do my writing, on a desk dwarfed by dunes of stuff. The desk is in fact an old teak table that Christie and I used to eat on in the apartments we shared, and then in the kitchen of our first house (we have a bigger kitchen table now).

Among the piles of baseball junk, alongside a Ted Lilly Pez dispenser, a half-dozen souvenir balls, several bobbleheads, and a small toy José Bautista, there's a ceramic liquor decanter, a promotional item from the James B. Beam Distilling Company of Clermont, Kentucky.

The decanter is oddly shaped, bell-like, with squarish shoulders and a narrow neck. Basically, it's a baseball that flares out just wide enough at the bottom to permit the whole thing to stand. Overtop the baseball, in small black, and large, faux-gilt lettering, are the words PROFESSIONAL BASEBALL'S 100TH ANNIVERSARY, and off to the sides the dates 1869 and 1969. Looming over all that is the image of a faceless right-handed batter who, having just struck the ball, is dropping his bat and surging forward out of the box toward first base. Printed on the back is the old lie about Abner Doubleday as the game's creator, and a mention of the Cincinnati Red Stockings as the first team of paid pros.

The bottle is itself now better than fifty years old. It came into my possession about fifteen years ago, and I'm unable to trace the chain of custody for its first thirty-five years of existence, except to say that whoever first owned it apparently purchased it in Wisconsin, according to the registered "State of" sticker planted on its flank.

The shape and design of the bottle evoke a time of large cars and pipe smoke, Earl Weaver and enormous ovoid stadiums with artificial turf, accessed by mounting concrete spiral ramps, like artless Guggenheims. There was a particular quality of light in such stadiums, somewhere between parking lot and arcade, and in their bowels lay ill-lit, circular corridors, stacked rings of them, all indistinguishable from one another. In their lifetime they represented several different things: progress, unity, artificiality, decline, blight. The bottle's like that: too big, devoid of real aesthetic charm, and harkening back to *olden days* in a manner that feels gestural and insincere.

⇢⇥⟞⟝⇤⇠

The decanter came into my hands empty and I've kept it that way. This, I reason, establishes it as an artifact and not a useful object. Useful objects are celebrated primarily for their usefulness, whereas artifacts can be celebrated for their temporal reach, their not-of-this-timeness.

Still, if I remove the cork stopper and lean over the opening, it smells faintly grainy, and there's a wisp of alcoholic tang. The scent leaves a dry, dusty, phantom sensation on my tongue, makes me think, "Yes, I *could* go for a drink."

It was a gift from my friend Paul. Paul has a habit of giving admirably thoughtful gifts. One birthday he also gifted me the Billy Ripken FUCK FACE card, for example, because he knew I'd love it for the way it smushed together childish humour and baseball history.

Paul and I met in grade school, were tight friends through high school and a couple of years of university, and remained close thereafter. He might be the most intelligent person I've ever known, with an aggressively restless curiosity that makes him dig into everything that catches his interest, and the intellectual capacity to haul it all in. A conversation with Paul darts from Bruce Lee's oeuvre to string theory to the history of fly fishing before you can settle yourself in your chair.

I didn't really touch alcohol or drugs in high school, but after graduating it was like I'd been let out of prison. Paul was right there with me. We started with tobacco in its appealing variety of forms, and found whisky right after that. We had tastes that ran from the louche to the high end, though God knows how we afforded any of it.

What I'm sure of is that we were using intoxicants to dip a toe into adulthood, making decisions regarding our own consciousness and wellbeing, choosing the poisons introduced into our bodies and owning the consequences. We might also have been equating these things with sophistication, or some barroom variant thereof. We used to go out after midnight, to the boardwalk through the Mer Bleue bog east of Ottawa, where the water was still and the air moved with croaks and hoots and the flapping of wings. We'd smoke cigars and take nips off a flask and talk until the light came.

In a shitty motel in Tucson we drank Serpent's Bite, a mashup of whisky and cider purchased at a nearby bullet-proof-glass-cloaked liquor store, and then passed out on the bathroom floor. We smoked cigarillos in Saguaro National Park, looking back over the city sunk in its bowl, shimmering in heat. Then we drove up to Seattle, gawking as we crawled by Kurt Cobain's house in a rented Oldsmobile. Cobain had been dead five years by then. I guess we wanted to know if there was a shrine.

I see Paul every few years now, and otherwise I'm terrible about keeping in touch. Life, you know. Kids. The usual. Excuses, really, but I'd like Paul to know that I miss him.

–»»«««–

Chief among the wonders of aging is the degree to which things change, suddenly and without warning. Scotch used to be my whisky of choice, but something changed. I still drink it when it's offered, but now I do so knowing that the next morning I will feel as though someone has placed a paperweight on my occipital lobe. I could take up rye, I suppose—I'm Canadian, after all. But I prefer bourbon, all of it—Bulleit or Maker's or Blanton's if someone else is paying, and Jim Beam if I am.

Not long ago I mixed an Old Fashioned with a heavy pour of Beam and I listened to the radio call as Vlad Guerrero Jr. hit his first homer in Toronto for the Blue Jays, and I thought about the time I drove with Paul to Montreal to see Tony Gwynn collect his 3,000th hit with the Padres while Vlad's father went 2-for-4 for the Expos. San Diego won 12–10. I was twenty-three years old. We drove home late at night and the world was large and wild, and I felt embryonic.

When I look at the Jim Beam commemorative baseball decanter, and I think about how old baseball is, about how old that decanter is, and about how old I am, and Paul is, and everything we've done, apart and together, the air around the thing starts to hum just a little. I become aware of the weight such objects acquire, and the gravity they come to exert on us, even if they are mass-produced promotional items, bits of plastic, frankly just junk. I think about our need to place upon these totems our own histories, our pain and our joy. Our need to make something human out of lifeless matter, which I'm going to venture is reducible to our fear of being alone.

All of which is to say: thanks, Paul, for the decanter, and the Billy Ripken card, and for baseball games, and for getting drunk with me when we were much younger and the whole world was still dizzying in its novelty.

# EVERY FIFTH DAY

The Seattle Mariners' history—notwithstanding Ichiro, Junior, Randy Johnson, Edgar Martínez, and the dazzling first seven years of Alex Rodriguez' career—is one long tale of woe studded with infrequently dazzling displays of capability, with all of it adding up to exactly zero championships. That those five brilliant players, and several other very good ones, have worn the trident or the compass and not known any postseason success seems either an injustice or an oversight on the part of whatever deities claim jurisdiction over the game. There's no logic to losing, just as there's no relief from the routine cruelties of time and money. Partisans feel the same way in Texas, of course, and in Milwaukee, and in San Diego too. But at least those teams have come close. Closer.

There is no greater embodiment of Seattle's legacy of unrewarded effort than Félix Hernández, who pitched his last game for the Mariners in 2019, at the listless end of another lost season. Félix spent fifteen seasons in Seattle and never once made the playoffs. In 2010 he was named the best pitcher in the American League while playing for a team that lost 101 games and finished 29 games behind the Rangers. Other than Ichiro, who that year collected 200 base hits for the tenth year in a row, Félix was the only bright spot in the Mariners roster. The gulf between personal accomplishment and team misery was never quite that bad again, but neither was it much better.

But every fifth day, there was Félix. He was good for about 30 starts a year, regularly logged in excess of 200 innings, and recorded more than 200 strikeouts every year from 2009 to 2014. Those all qualify as elite numbers in a very competitive field. But that was Félix—reliably brilliant, tucked away in the Pacific Northwest, putting in the work, every fifth day, for fifteen years. Everybody knew he was up there, doing his thing, but few watched all that closely. For those fifteen years, the Mariners were seldom the sort of team likely to be shown on a nationally televised game.

At the Rogers Centre in Toronto you can get seats in the outfield right over the bullpens. I sat above the visitors' pen for a game during his 2010 Cy Young Award season, and got to my seat early enough to watch him warm up before the first pitch. He was so fluid, so mechanically flawless, and the sound his pitches made thocking into the bullpen catcher's glove seemed to probe some thoracic concavity I hadn't been aware I possessed. He went out that afternoon and one-hit the Blue Jays, giving up just a solo homer—José Bautista's 50th of the year—and lost 1–0. That about summed up his season—heroic in the face of defeat, often looking like the only competent one in his side's uniform.

He remained consistently dazzling until 2016, when the miles started to take their toll on the chassis. The engine remained good, but structural weaknesses had crept in, the result of hard wear over the years, and would not be willed away. Three arduous years later, at the end of a contract, earning too much money, with the Mariners again facing what's charitably termed a "rebuild," there was no place for him on the team. This is the harsh economy of both baseball and life, where loyalty and service are unequal to the other, unfeeling side of the ledger, and so change is deemed necessary, even if it isn't desired by anyone willing to say as much in a public forum.

But everything wound down, and on the final Thursday night of that end-of-contract season he was due to start against Oakland. Nobody in a position to offer him a new contract was willing to state with certainty that it was his last game in a Seattle uniform, but it didn't take tea leaves to read the future. This was his swan song, and everyone knew it.

There are a million different things that might link us to the players we take as our own, why certain guys end up our favourites. Félix was a neck-tattooed Venezuelan whose emotions bubbled barely beneath the skin; I'm a pale Canadian with the reserve to match. There's a decade separating us. And yet I felt emotionally bound up in his career. By that I mean that I didn't just enjoy the way he pitched; I felt a kinship with him, some kind of attachment that is absent when I consider 99.9 percent of other big-league ballplayers.

That's the closest I can come to explaining why I dressed up in my Félix jersey and M's cap, made popcorn, and chilled a six-pack ahead of his last Mariners appearance, which wouldn't start until my Eastern time zone bedtime.

I watched Félix struggle through the first inning, wherein he walked two batters and surrendered a base hit that scored a run. My heart ached with the knowledge that time is implacable and will claim us all as he gave up a two-run homer in the second inning. I drank four Old Milwaukee tallboys. I kept a scorecard. I cheered—out loud, though the rest of the family was asleep upstairs—for each of his three strikeouts, and I cried—fully bawled—as he did when his manager came out and relieved him of his duties with one out in the sixth inning. I cried in a way that certain grown men feel permitted to do when someone in a baseball uniform does something beautiful, or unprecedented, or does anything for the last time. Félix cried in a way you don't often see an athlete emote. It was so plainly and beautifully human.

And that, I now think to myself, is probably what made Félix Hernández so appealing. He was a kid when he arrived, nineteen and seemingly overawed by the flash and heat of big-league life. Though he was good, that was clear. Better maybe than the Mariners deserved, if they weren't going to build a winner around him. But for fifteen years he maintained a loyalty to the fanbase and the organization that was first loyal to him, and when half that equation suddenly disappeared— when the Baseball Club of Seattle, LP, deemed his services insufficient to justify further compensation—he hurt, and he cried in public. And in that way, I think, he's one of us, caught in the mechanisms of late capitalism's asymmetrical exchange, giving away our best years, showing more loyalty than we ourselves are shown by the institutions and employers and brands and bodies that crowd our lives, even if we're capable of uncommon brilliance every fifth day.

# A MEANS OF COPING

If you use baseball to mark the seasons, late winter's longer days would, under normal circumstances, portend the last few stress-free days of spring training and the imminence of Opening Day, the moment of deliverance from our long period of privation.

But the spring of 2020 was not normal: the novel coronavirus was racing across the world, popping up in country after country. It would soon begin a nearly unimpeded spread throughout the United States. Sports, like most other aspects of what we had come to know as regular life, were put on hold. Spring training ground to a halt, and the question became not when the regular season would begin, but if.

On the list of possible tragedies, the loss of live baseball does not rank. But what 2020 brought to me and my family was a mixture of anxiety and boredom. There was time to kill as we stayed at home, avoided others, and washed our hands. I filled some of the void by reading about baseball, which helped a bit. But books could not replace the way that baseball, when all's going as it should, fills in the cracks that emerge throughout the day, which I typically soundtrack with a background game. Making dinner, cleaning the dishes, whatever. The TV's reassuring glow, the announcers' voices, the crowd's reedy murmur, the sweet, utterly ignorable presence of it.

In the absence of anything resembling the commonplace, I found myself reaching into my bag for the trick that gets me through winter's coldest, darkest, most remote days: plumbing the depths of YouTube for old ball games to watch, listen to, ignore. That there was no live baseball on the horizon only lent the act a greater urgency.

With luck, as you read this you're not confined to your house or apartment for the umpteenth month on end. Perhaps it's winter, or the All-Star break. Or maybe it's four in the morning and you just need a baseball fix. Whatever the exact details of your situation, the modern world provides the digital means to lessen the symptoms. The prescription is YouTube. To get started, type "NBC GOW" into the search box and unlock a few decades' worth of *Game of the Week* broadcasts, distant Saturday afternoons encased in digital amber.

"...and that's in there," says Vin Scully of a Jack Morris fastball humming by Carlton Fisk. It's April 1984, early in the Tigers' incredible run at the beginning of their championship season. Morris is just beginning to no-hit Tony LaRussa's White Sox. Big Greg Luzinski ("Here comes a butter and egg man," says Vin) puts his weight behind a Morris offering and knocks it toward centre, only to have the Chicago breeze nudge it down where it settles into Chet Lemon's glove.

Or jump back a few years to watch the South Siders in their goofy collared uniforms take on Jim Clancy and the Blue Jays in August 1980. Harry Caray on the call, sharing Marine Corps jokes off air with his colour man, Jimmy Piersall, the two chuckling knowingly when they return from ninety seconds of Miller Lite and Oldsmobile and Sears commercials, theirs a private, jocular conversation that viewers only happen to hear.

An instalment of ABC's *Monday Night Baseball* from June 1976 has Billy Martin and the Yankees in Detroit to face the Tigers behind their eccentric rookie and sudden pitching star Mark Fidrych. Near the top of the broadcast the Yanks introduce themselves.

"Roy White, left field, Wayne, New Jersey," says the leadoff man, looking straight into the camera.

"Uh, Oscar Gamble, right field, Montgomery, Alabama," says the man with the most famous afro in baseball history.

"Billy Martin, manager," says the embattled skipper, "Born: Berkeley, California. Died: New York."

On the end of another link the Seattle Pilots steal one on a Sunday afternoon at Fenway, thanks to eight-plus strong innings from Mike Marshall. It'll be one of 64 wins the Pilots will collect in their only season of existence.

To wade through the videos on offer is to trace eras of announcing (Red Barber's southern loquaciousness, Bob Prince's stern verbal stenography, Caray's lubricated looseness, and Vin—timeless Vin), the history of fashion (Tony Kubek doing pregame interviews in a riotous sports coat), and changes in the game (gone are the exuberant windmill delivery, bloused pants, the extended stirrup with tight pants and pullover jersey, the ponderous ritual of the pitchout).

For all its prideful stubbornness, baseball has evolved, but in the virtual stream it becomes an ahistorical soup, the 1977 Yankees rubbing up against the 2001 Mariners and the '68 Cardinals. We Are Family and the Big Red Machine and the Cardiac Kids and the Amazin's and Nos Amours. Exhibitions, early-season snoozers, All-Star Games, World Series nail-biters. In YouTube's chronological blender, Ken Griffey Jr. is always chugging around third on Edgar's double to beat the Yankees, Mark Fidrych is always a goofy, charismatic rookie phenom on the rise, and Ichiro is always delivering a long-distance precision strike to nab Terrence Long at third. Picture quality careens from black-and-white abstraction to grainy videotape—but it's all baseball, and in our moments of need that's all it has to be.

Here, on offer at all hours to anyone with internet access, resides the shapeless, casual joy of time-hopping between events of no great consequence. When the world convulses under the strain of traumatic events, there's decadence to be found in triviality.

Some of the videos were posted by an arm on MLB's vast organizational chart, but most seem to have been uploaded by individual hobbyists operating under clunky pseudonyms. There's a sense, when sifting through this archive, that the videos all rest on precarious ground. MLB is concerned primarily, I don't need to tell you, with protecting its property and profits. Surely only anonymity or scale protects the posters—the puniness of those responsible for uploading converted VHS dubs to YouTube's limitless body has led them to be overlooked by the massive and ungainly body responsible for the ownership and steerage of big-league baseball. Whatever the cause, whether legal lassitude, corporate benevolence, or pesky contractual loophole, let's agree that it's in our collective interest that these artifacts persist free of charge for as long as possible.

The NBC broadcasts of Games Six and Seven of the 1952 Yankees–Dodgers classic are the oldest complete World Series TV broadcasts we have, and they're a treat. Mel Allen narrates the action during Game Seven, the Yankees up 4–2 in the bottom of the seventh. "The grim determination on Billy's face, the seriousness of the situation, exemplified and revealed beautifully by our fine cameras," says Allen as Dodger third baseman Billy Cox stands in against Vic Raschi. Cox slaps a base hit to right, moving Carl Furillo to second, and bringing up Pee Wee Reese—"spark plug of the Dodgers," Allen calls him, "the captain, the little colonel"—with Duke Snider waiting in the on-deck circle.

With one out and the count at 3–1, home-plate ump Larry Goetz calls Raschi's rib-tickler a strike. Reese was ready to take his base. "Got the inside corner," says Allen charitably. "Man alive, this crowd is ready to roar." The next pitch is low—low enough even for Goetz—and the bases are loaded.

Casey Stengel strides out to the mound and gives Raschi the hook, bringing in the lefty Bob Kuzava, who Allen describes with almost taxonomic precision: "From Wyandotte, Michigan, a six-foot-two, two hundred pounder, blue eyes, blond hair." All this to fill air time while Kuzava throws his warm-up pitches.

Late afternoon shadows envelop the pitcher and batter. Snider works the count full. The sun draws Ebbets Field's roof in a wavy crenellated line between the mound and second, the silhouette of a flag flaps near the shortstop's position. Snider swings mightily but pops weakly to Gil McDougald at third with the infield fly rule in effect, and no runners advance. Jackie Robinson comes up with two out.

In 2020 these were my scruffy efforts to maintain something distracting, something pointlessly beautiful and human, as the world seemed to crumble around us. But the world has crumbled before, and baseball's still here, just as it will be when everything settles down again.

Robinson fouls the first pitch off. "And the Dodgers in the dugout, tense with anxiety," says Allen, "and in the Yankee dugout they're tense with anxiety."

At 2–1 Jackie pulls a fly ball that lands up on the ballpark's roof, but foul. Stengel springs out of the Yankee dugout to follow the ball's path, marvelling at its distance. After another, less impressive foul ball, Robinson waves at Kuzava's next pitch and sends the ball squibbing into the Flatbush sky. It's set to fall into no-man's-land behind the mound, despite the charging efforts of every New York infielder. But at the last second, a lunging Billy Martin streaks in from second and catches the ball at his shoetops. "And how about that!" says Allen, utilizing his trademark phrase. "Man, it's been a great Series," he continues, "it still is. We've got two more innings at least to go," which, in the spring of that awful year, were just about the most comforting words I could imagine.

In late winter I am generally prone to an itchy impatience. The long nights, the short days, the lack of baseball, they all conspire against me. The membrane separating my ability to cope from my sometimes paralyzing anxiety wears thinner by the day. I try to imagine doing something useful. Universally acknowledged all-time great Bill Russell suffered anxiety so acute that he threw up before nearly every game, and yet he still managed to score 14,500 points and win 11 NBA championships. Where do I get myself some of that ability to deal?

I've leaned on a number of techniques over the years, with varying levels of effectiveness. Music is reliable, as is exercise, but I'm always looking for additional tools to add to the box, and when I find one I tend to wield it until it no longer possesses the power to calm me. I have used, in no particular order: scented candles; herbal tea; a digital nature sound generator, including (most soothingly) that of crickets; and, most recently, a video loop shot from the locomotive of a train passing through the serene, snowy Norwegian countryside. I used it for most of one fall and winter, believing it to be a live video feed. Something about that thrilled me. Only toward spring did I recognize that certain scenes were repeating themselves. Still, the footage cooled my blood.

Christie, the wildlife biologist, who weathers these tools of mine with good humour and inhuman patience (she found the crickets particularly irritating), passed my monitor one morning and, watching as the train passed through a forested swath of Norway, asked, "Has it hit a moose yet?"

Perhaps surprisingly, one thing that has not diminished in its ability to bring me comfort is astronomy. I locate solace in considering the unfathomable size of the universe, especially news of discoveries that enlarge human understanding of our own cosmic insignificance. There's wonder in that, the kind I knew as a kid, when I would lie in the grass with a hand-me-down Walkman, headphones piping Carl Sagan's voice into my ears as he took me on a "Star Walk," instructing me to look "three hand widths above the southern horizon to locate Sirius, or the Dog Star."

So I was excited when, late in 2018, as the days grew darker and colder, a team of researchers from the European Southern Observatory published a paper identifying a proto-supercluster of galaxies they named Hyperion. They suggested Hyperion is roughly five thousand times the size of the Milky Way, with a mass in excess of one million billion times that of the sun, and sits about eleven billion light years from Earth.

I read the paper, and understood some of it. I gazed at the cold winter sky and within my very limited abilities I marvelled at the scope and structure of the cosmos. The galaxies viewed within Hyperion were young when the visible light was sent out into the universe, and as we speak they continue in their evolution into stable star clusters. From Earth, they are dim specks barely visible within the very small constellation of Sextans. They form one of the largest structures in the universe, but you can't really see them.

The thought of Hyperion and the excitement it bred in me carried me through much of that winter, until it was announced that Ichiro Suzuki, inactive for most of the 2018 season but not officially retired, would be on the Seattle Mariners' roster for the first two games of the 2019 season. Then I started thinking of baseball pretty much all the time.

From his MLB debut in 2001, Ichiro was an echo, a glimpse of a universe distinct from the one we inhabit, visible but unreachable. He played his own game. He slapped base hits. He dropped drag bunts up the line. He ran. He scrapped. For all this, he inspired wonder.

And then in May 2018, no longer a major-league-calibre player, he transitioned into a non-playing role, but vowed he'd return to spring training the following year to attempt to crack the lineup.

In August, when the schedule for the 2019 season was released, the baseball internet was quick to notice that it featured an Opening Series—two games between the Seattle Mariners and the Oakland Athletics to be held in Tokyo, a full two weeks before the rest of the teams began their slate. Two things were by then clear: first, that the Mariners, with an assist from Major League Baseball, were determined to give Ichiro a fitting send-off, and second, that they were similarly determined to remove him from the regular roster thereafter. This, it seemed, was the perfect solution, allowing all parties to save face.

Baseball has opened its season in Tokyo before, and in Australia, and regular season contests have also been staged in Mexico City, Monterrey, San Juan, and London. The 2019 Tokyo opener wasn't the first attempt to showcase the product to international audiences. But it seemed to be the first time they'd engineered the schedule to honour one particular player. Ichiro's standing in the game was so rare that he merited such treatment. It was to be a spectacle staged for maximum pageantry, but also it was fitting; a strange game in an unusual place for possibly the most unique superstar ever to play in the major leagues.

→→⟨⟨←

In Greek myth according to Hesiod, Hyperion was a Titan, son of Uranus and Gaia. The name itself means "High One" or "Watcher from Above." Hyperion wed his sister, Theia, and their son Helios created the sun. Their daughters, Eos and Selene, gave us dawn and the moon, respectively. Hyperion was among the Titans who overthrew Uranus (including

Hyperion's brother, Cronos, who castrated their father) in order to rule over a Golden Age, until they were themselves tossed aside by the Olympians, led by Cronos's son, Zeus.

※

In Japanese baseball culture, preparation is key. There are some who believe that the more strenuous the training, the better. "The purpose of training," wrote Suisha Tobita, "is the forging of the soul. If the players do not try so hard as to vomit blood in practice, they cannot hope to win games. One must suffer to be good." Ichiro's father agreed, and gave his son a glove when the boy was three. Daily workouts began when he was in the third grade. When the elder Suzuki handed his son off to high school coaches, he instructed them to be tough. "No matter how good Ichiro is, don't ever praise him," he said. "We have to make him spiritually strong." The father-son relationship, Ichiro has said, "bordered on hazing." "Child abuse" is another term he's used. The son eventually cast off the father, and now the two do not speak.

※

The 2019 winter passed. Spring training came. Ichiro reported. The Mariners were scheduled to play a month's worth of exhibition games before heading to Japan. The roster would swell to include enough fresh bodies to minimize the strain of trans-Pacific travel. Ichiro would, of course, be in uniform.

As the teams boarded charters in Arizona, Ichiro had yet to announce his retirement. He admitted to nothing but a desire to play, and to help his team.

On the morning of the first scheduled game I woke early, as I usually do, but instead of setting to work, I sat with a coffee cup in my hand and watched the Mariners and the A's.

All the ghosts were present. Ichiro was still built as he was when he debuted: wiry, lean, quick-limbed. His swing was the same, he still ran and caught and threw the same way. But the hits didn't come as they used to. The infield dribblers he used to beat out now resulted in outs. His bat struggled to catch up to fastballs. Breaking stuff vexed him. He looked good in the field in a pair of exhibition games against the Yomiuri Giants, but went hitless with a walk in the first game against Oakland, a contest the Mariners won 9–7.

The last of Ichiro's 3,604 professional games was the next morning, and I was again up to watch it. Batting ninth, he flew out in the second inning, and grounded out to the second baseman in the fourth.

By the time the game had reached the later innings, the rest of my family was up and busy getting ready for school and work. At breakfast, maybe seven-thirty or so, I set the laptop on the table, and the kids and I watched as we ate.

There was a lot to appreciate in that ultimate game, not least of which the fact that the final score—5–4 Seattle in extras—mirrored the score by which the Mariners beat the A's in Ichiro's stateside debut in 2001. There was also his beautiful and heartfelt performance in the post-game press conference, conducted entirely in Japanese and later translated into English, which included a brief exchange with a reporter that captured perfectly what it was about Ichiro, beyond the physical beauty of the way he played the game, that made him so compelling a figure for so long. When asked if he would like to tell fans about his "philosophy of life," Ichiro replied:

> *I don't know much about a philosophy of life, but when I think of it as the way I go through life... As I said earlier, I can't work harder than everyone else. Right until the end, you are only measured against yourself. As you do that, as you see your limits, you try over and over to surpass yourself a tiny bit. That's how I eventually become*

*who I am. One can only do this in small increments, but that is the way to surpass yourself. If you try and change in leaps and bounds, that gap between where you are (and your target) becomes too large and I think unsustainable, so the only way is the steady way.*

In his final at-bat—the last of 14,832 professional plate appearances over twenty-eight seasons split between Japan's Pacific League and Major League Baseball—he grounded out to the shortstop in the top of the eighth inning, and was removed from the field by manager Scott Servais in the bottom of the frame, jogging off to adulatory applause, greeted at the dugout steps by teammates to exchange hugs in a goodbye that halted the game for several minutes.

Dee Gordon had tears in his eyes. Seattle starter Yusei Kikuchi—making his Major League debut—wept openly. Ken Griffey Jr., who'd travelled with the team for the occasion, met Ichiro in the dugout and wrapped him in a bear hug.

It's Ichiro's second-to-last at-bat, though, with none out and a runner on second in the top of the seventh, which lingers.

Thinking he might be pulled early, and that this might therefore be his final plate appearance, we stood around the kitchen table to watch it, the three kids, aged nine to twelve, Christie, and me. If there was an overbearing sense of portent to that scene, I suppose it must've been the product of time and familiarity. I have watched Ichiro longer than my children have been alive. Christie and I first saw him live on our first long road trip together, eighteen years earlier. My children knew his name before they knew Babe Ruth or Hank Aaron or Aaron Judge. He was a constant presence in our household—in our lives—for almost two decades. It was hard in that moment, and remains difficult now, to imagine not only baseball but my life without him.

After falling behind 0–2, Ichiro worked the count back to 2–2. And then one more time he stepped in, raised his right arm, and willed the moment into stillness, the bat perfectly upright. He tugged at his jersey's shoulder with his left hand, then coiled to await the pitch.

A's reliever Joakim Soria reared and dealt.

Ichiro watched the pitch come in, a breaking ball that buckled his knees just a little bit. He let the ball sail by, as though he couldn't quite undertake the decisive action, the years exerting their cumulative weight on him, the necessary muscle twitch just a fraction of a fraction of a second slower than it had once been.

A called third strike, attended by a kind of shock—"Oh!" said the citizens of Tokyo, collectively—followed by a slim second of silence as they tried to reconcile what they had seen with what they had desired. The applause came gradually thereafter, and was polite, solemn.

It should only have been a gentle disappointment—it was, after all, the most statistically probable outcome—and yet I was crestfallen. Across its history, baseball has been generous with its drama, perhaps to a fault. It instills a stubborn hope, one that wriggles with insistence even when, or especially when, the odds suggest no celebration is in the offing. It makes one believe again and again that the impossible might be coddled into extending its blessing onto a favourite team or player, just this once. Watch long enough, many of us insist, and the fantastic becomes not only feasible but likely. That, ultimately, is what keeps us watching.

I'd have traded all of the game's exhilarating and storied moments—Babe calling his shot, Mazeroski downing the Yankees at Forbes Field, Joe Carter winning the Series, you name it—to have a flake of that rare magic settle on Ichiro's bat one last time.

But no such charm visited him, or us. The umpire made his call. The catcher fired the ball back to the pitcher. The lights in the Tokyo Dome burned on. The stars continued along their prescribed paths. The hundred thousand galaxies within Hyperion churned onward toward a maturity no human will ever witness.

Ichiro stood for a breath, the camera trained on his face, which betrayed perhaps the weakest hint of disbelief, and then he walked mutely back to the dugout and took his seat.

As he made for the bench, the woman I married, having stalled her daily preparations, making it likely she'd be late for work, stood next to me, and though she will deny it I swear to you there was a tear in her eye. Finally, she broke our silence and said, quietly, "That looked a little high to me."

## ACKNOWLEDGEMENTS

I am indebted to many more people than I can name, but I wish to specifically thank and credit the following:

For information on Ichiro in particular, and Japanese and Asian baseball in general, I have leaned heavily on the work of Robert K. Fitts, Joseph A. Reaves, Robert Whiting, and Wright Thompson's and Chris Jones's writing for ESPN.

Thanks to Jeeho Yoo for guidance with Korean naming conventions.

Finishing the piece now known as "Spoke, Peck, and the Greatest Baseball Game Ever Played in Peterborough" required a great deal of digging, and I was abetted in that work by a good many people and organizations, including Cassidy Lent at the Giamatti Research Center at the National Baseball Hall of Fame and Museum in Cooperstown; Jenn Bennett of the Municipality of Marmora and Lake and the Marmora Historical Foundation; Jon Oldham, archivist for the City of Peterborough; the staff at the Peterborough Public Library; the Peterborough and District Sports Hall of Fame; the Kawartha Ancestral Research Association; *Peterborough Examiner* contributor Pat Marchen; the art installation "Company Town" by Anne White, Ann Jaeger, Miranda Gee Jones, Lillian Ross-Millard, and Eryn Lidster, exhibited at Peterborough Artspace, July 13–19, 2020, and online at companytown.ca.

I also consulted the following monographs: Charles C. Alexander, *Spoke: A Biography of Tris Speaker* (SMU Press, 2007); Timothy M. Gay, *Tris Speaker: The Rough-and-Tumble Life of a Baseball Legend* (University of Nebraska Press, 2005); William Humber, *Diamonds of the North: A Concise History of Baseball in Canada* (Oxford UP, 1995); Ian S. Kahanowitz,

*Baseball Gods in Scandal: Cobb, Speaker, and the Dutch Leonard Affair* (Summer Game Books, 2019); Curt Smith, *Storied Stadiums: Baseball's History Through Its Ballparks* (Da Capo Press, 2001).

Scott Martelle's *Detroit: A Biography* (Chicago Review Press, 2012) provided context and historical information for "Love in the Time of."

For general information, including rosters, box scores, uniform histories, and records, I made extensive use of Baseball Reference (baseball-reference.com), Retrosheet (retrosheet.org), Dressed to the Nines (exhibits.baseballhalloffame.org/dressed_to_the_nines/database.htm), and the Society for American Baseball Research (sabr.org), particularly the BioProject Committee's work on Pedro Guerrero (written by Frank Morris), Roger Peckinpaugh (written by Peter M. Gordon), George Sisler (written by Bill Lamberty), and Tris Speaker (written by Don Jensen).

Some of the pieces in the preceding pages first appeared in fragments or varying forms online or in print, and I'm grateful for the opportunities and the editorial guidance provided by the following: Aaron Burch at *Hobart*; Eric Fershtman at *Sinkhole Magazine*; Justin Hargett at *Eephus*; Joanne Hulbert at *Turnstyle: The SABR Journal of Baseball Arts*; Rachael McDaniel at *The Hardball Times*; Jason Schwartz at *The SABR Baseball Cards Blog*; and Chris Toman at *VICE Canada*.

Thanks to the Ontario Arts Council for a Recommender Grant which made possible the writing of this book.

For local support, thank you to Michelle Berry, Lewis MacLeod, and Trent University. For critical insight early in the life of this book, I'm indebted to Rob Winger.

A huge and hearty thank you to my editor, Andrew Faulkner, whose fascination with the game's minutiae mirrors my own, and whose organizational mind puts mine to shame. Working with an editor like you doesn't feel like work at all. Let's do it again sometime, again.

Enormous and ongoing gratitude to Leigh Nash, whose courage and energy inspires. Thanks for the chance to do this once more.

Big thanks to the rest of the Invisible team, including Megan Fildes for her wonderful designs, and to Julie Wilson, who is tireless and creative in their efforts to get their authors' work out into the world.

Deepest gratitude and love to Mom and Dad, Robyn, Peter, and their families, and to Sharron and John and all the Curleys. Special thanks are reserved for Adelaide, Cormac, and Theo for their enthusiasm and curiosity, for games of catch, for justifying my renewed interest in baseball cards, and for help with an eleventh-hour fact-check. And thanks, finally, to Christie. Always Christie.

INVISIBLE PUBLISHING produces fine Canadian literature for those who enjoy such things. As an independent, not-for-profit publisher, our work includes building communities that sustain and encourage engaging, literary, and current writing.

Invisible Publishing has been in operation for over a decade. We released our first fiction titles in the spring of 2007, and our catalogue has come to include works of graphic fiction and non-fiction, pop culture biographies, experimental poetry, and prose.

We are committed to publishing diverse voices and experiences. In acknowledging historical and systemic barriers, and the limits of our existing catalogue, we strongly encourage writers from LGBTQ2SIA+ communities, Indigenous writers, and writers of colour to submit their work.

Invisible Publishing is also home to the Bibliophonic series of music books and the Throwback series of CanLit reissues.

If you'd like to know more, please get in touch: info@invisiblepublishing.com